COOLCROCHET

30 HOT, FUN DESIGNS TO CROCHET AND WEAR

MELISSA LEAPMAN

PHOTOGRAPHY BY JOE VANDEHATERT

WATSON-GUPTILL PUBLICATIONS / NEW YORK

FOR MARK, WHO KNOWS ALL ABOUT BEING
COOL

Senior Acquisitions Editor: Joy Aquilino
Project Editor: Andrea Curley
Book Designer: Barbara Balch
Production Manager: Hector Campbell
Technical Editor: Laura Polley
Principal photography: Joe VanDeHatert
Sweater closeups and details photography: Milt Crosson
Charts and schematic illustrations: Melissa Leapman
Instructional illustrations: Sherry Polley

First published in 2005 by Watson-Guptill Publications,
a division of VNU Business Media, Inc.,
770 Broadway, New York, N.Y. 10003
www.wgpub.com

Library of Congress Cataloging-in-Publication Data
Leapman, Melissa.
  Cool crochet : 30 hot, fun designs to crochet and wear /
Melissa Leapman ;
photography by Joe VanDeHatert.
    p. cm.
  Includes bibliographical references and index.
  ISBN 0-8230-1124-0 (alk. paper)
  1. Crocheting--Patterns. 2. Clothing and dress. 3. Dress
accessories. I. Title.
  TT825.L3863 2005
  746.43'40432--dc22
2004030279

ACKNOWLEDGMENTS

I'd like to thank the following talented individuals for
testing the patterns and creating the samples for this book:
Brenda Allred, Denise Augostine, Marianne Forrestal,
Toni Gill, Cindy Grosch, Kim Guzman, Barbara Hillery,
Jodi Lewanda, Ritu Mehrotra, JoAnn Moss, Joyce Pearson,
Laura Polley, Barbara Pretzsch, Sharon Ryman, Rusty Slabinski,
Sereta Vallo, and Renee Wissbroecker.

I am especially grateful to every company that generously
supplied materials. Your beautiful products have provided me
with tremendous inspiration (and lots of pleasure!) throughout
my design career.

Special thanks go to my editors, Joy Aquilino and Andrea
Curley, for their over-the-top professionalism and dedication
to this project.

Finally, to Laura Polley, my wonderful tech editor, thank
you for your careful attention to all the little details. And
don't worry, a new telephone is already on order!

ABBREVIATIONS

approx — approximately
bead ch — bead chain
beg — begin(ning)
BPDC — back post double crochet
BPTR — back post triple crochet
ch(s) — chain(s)
ch sp — chain space
cm — centimeter(s)
cont — continu(e)(ing)
dc — double crochet
dec — decreas(e)(ing)
dtr — double triple crochet
FPDC — front post double crochet
FPDTR — front post double triple crochet
FPTR — front post triple crochet
hdc — half double crochet
inc — increas(e)(ing)

LH — left-hand
mm — millimeter(s)
mult — multiple(s)
oz — ounce(s)
patt(s) — pattern(s)
rem — remain(ing)
RH — right-hand
rnd(s) — round(s)
RS — right side
sc — single crochet
sp(s) — space(s)
st(s) — stitch(es)
tog — together
tr — triple crochet
WS — wrong side
yd — yard(s)

PATTERN SYMBOLS

* — repeat instructions after asterisk or between asterisks across row or for as many times as instructed
( ) — repeat instructions within parentheses for as many times as instructed
___ — placeholder for size(s) to which specific instructions do not pertain

Note: American terms are used throughout this book. For terms that have different U.K. equivalents, see table opposite. Instructions for Basic Stitches, Stitch Variations, Assembly Instructions, and Finishing Techniques begin on page 124.

AMERICAN TERM	U.K. TERM
double crochet (dc)	treble crochet (tr)
double triple crochet (dtr)	triple treble crochet (tr tr)
gauge	tension
half double crochet (hdc)	half treble crochet (htr)
single crochet (sc)	double crochet (dc)
slip stitch	single crochet (sc)
triple crochet (tr)	double treble crochet (dtr)
yarn over	yarn over hook

YARN CHOICE AND SUBSTITUTION

I've designed each project in this collection for a specific yarn. Due to unique characteristics such as fiber content, twist, texture, and thickness, every yarn appears and behaves differently when crocheted. Therefore, for the best results, I recommend that you use the suggested yarn.

If you would like to make a yarn substitution, be sure to choose one whose weight matches the one designated in the pattern. Crochet a swatch of solid single crochet with the yarn you prefer, using the hook size suggested on the ball band, and count the number of stitches over 4". Refer to the table opposite to determine its weight.

Before beginning any project, take the time to crochet a gauge swatch as recommended in the pattern and carefully measure your gauge. When making the actual project, use the size crochet hook you require to obtain the gauge specified in the pattern.

YARN WEIGHT	STITCHES PER 4"
Fingering weight	24 or more
Sport weight	22-24
Light worsted weight	20-22
Worsted weight	19-20
Heavy worsted weight	16-18
Bulky weight	15 or fewer

Contents

DARLA 66
Advanced
*Cotton/Lycra®
wrap top*

JULIANNA 70
Advanced
*Cardigan with
¾-length sleeves*

VALENTINA 76
Advanced Beginner
Openwork stole

PENINA 79
Advanced
*Cropped bolero-style
jacket*

ILENE 84
Advanced
*Geometric-patterned
pullover*

NANCY 88
Advanced Beginner
*Casual fleece
pullover*

CASSIE 92
Advanced Beginner
Striped linen tote

NATALIE 96
Advanced Beginner
*Halter with ties and
beaded edging*

ANDREA 99
Intermediate
Hip drawstring bag

HOLLY 102
Intermediate
*Openwork tunic
with side slits*

PATTI 106
Advanced
*Aran-style panel
pullover*

MARGO 111
Advanced Beginner
String bikini

TRACI 114
Intermediate
Cozy cloche hat

TONI 116
Intermediate
*Textured raglan
pullover*

ANIKA 120
Intermediate
*Pullover with
bell sleeves*

Introduction

The mere mention of the word "crochet" typically conjures up sentimental images of exquisite, ecru-colored family heirlooms or cozy, handmade afghans and other home dec items.

But savvy stitchers know—and trend watchers are quick to agree—that these same crochet techniques are being used to create **up-to-the-minute** garments and fashion accessories. *(Not only do many celebrities and New York City models strut along ritzy red carpets and fashion runways wearing beautiful crocheted pieces, they tuck crocheted works-in-progress inside their tote bags, too!)*

For this new collection, I've designed thirty **fun and fresh** projects

- to combine this cherished craft with today's **hottest** fashion trends. *(Envision flowing, openwork bell sleeves on an otherwise opaque sweater or a marled off-the-shoulder pullover, form fitting and fabulous.)*

- to offer crocheters **fun-to-make** projects that fit perfectly into their wardrobes and lifestyles. *(Why buy something that's factory-made when you can happily make it yourself—and be able to choose your favorite color to boot?)*

- to showcase the **newest,** most **exciting** yarns on the market. *(Sometimes, it's okay to just let the yarn do all the work.)*

- to add whimsy—and even some **glitz!**—to your project wishlist. *(Chances are you won't save the glittery red pullover for special occasions only!)*

■ to provide patterns for **hip** gifts you can make for your fashion-conscious friends. *(To me, accessories such as trendy hats and bags are a lot like shoes: You can never own too many!)*

My grandmother taught me how to crochet when I was a toddler. I'll bet she never imagined what would eventually fly off my hook—let alone that I'd author entire books of designs! Some of these projects may surprise you too. You might even wonder if a few are actually crocheted. Nonetheless, all of these designs—from the sparkly crystal and wire necklace to the Aran-inspired pullover, from the funky bouclé clutch to the ribbed A-line duster—use those same **basic crochet techniques** lovingly passed on from generation to generation.

Aren't we lucky that crochet is an **art form** that's evolved along with our modern sensibility?

Today's crochet is . . . Cool Crochet!

Elisabeth

Soft and flirty, this shaped pullover features a fun loop edging.

GAUGE

In Solid Hdc Patt, 18 sts and 12 rows = 4". To measure your gauge, make a test swatch as follows: Ch 19. Work Solid Hdc Patt on 18 sts for 12 rows total. Fasten off. Piece should measure 4" square. **To save time, take time to check gauge.**

SOLID HALF DOUBLE CROCHET PATTERN

(any number of sts)

Foundation Row (RS): Hdc into third ch from hook and into each ch across. Ch 2, turn.

Patt Row: Skip first hdc, *hdc into next hdc. Repeat from * across, ending row with hdc into top of turning-ch-2. Ch 2, turn.

Repeat Patt Row for patt.

NOTES

Throughout, each hdc, dec hdc, and turning-ch-2 counts as 1 st.

To increase 1 st each side, ch 2 to turn; skip first st, 2 hdc into next st; hdc into each st across until 2 sts rem, ending row with 2 hdc into next st, hdc into top of turning-ch-2. Ch 2, turn.

To decrease 1 st each side, ch 2 to turn; skip first st, work a dec hdc to combine next 2 sts; hdc into each st across until 3 sts rem, ending row with dec hdc to combine next 2 sts, hdc into top of turning-ch-2. Ch 2, turn.

Continued on next page.

BACK

Ch 70 (76, 84, 92, 100, 108).

Beg Solid Hdc Patt, and work even on 69 (75, 83, 91, 99, 107) sts for 2 rows. Ch 2, turn.

Shape Body

Next Row (RS): Skip first hdc, hdc into next 22 (25, 29, 33, 37, 41) sts, 2 hdc into next st, hdc into next 21 sts, 2 hdc into next st, hdc into each st across to end row—71 (77, 85, 93, 101, 109) sts.

Cont even in patt as established for 3 rows.

Next Row (RS): Skip first hdc, hdc into next 22 (25, 29, 33, 37, 41) sts, 2 hdc into next st, hdc into next 23 sts, 2 hdc into next st, hdc into each st across to end row—73 (79, 87, 95, 103, 111) sts.

Cont even in patt as established for 3 rows.

Next Row (RS): Skip first hdc, hdc into next 22 (25, 29, 33, 37, 41) sts, 2 hdc into next st, hdc into next 25 sts, 2 hdc into next st, hdc into each st across to end row—75 (81, 89, 97, 105, 113) sts.

Cont even in patt as established for 3 rows.

SKILL LEVEL
Intermediate

SIZES
Small (Medium, Large, Extra-Large, Extra-Extra-Large, Extra-Extra-Extra Large). *Instructions are for smallest size, with changes for other sizes noted in parentheses as necessary.*

FINISHED MEASUREMENTS
Bust: 34 (37, 40½, 44, 47½, 51)"
Total length (excluding edging): 20 (20½, 21, 21½, 22, 22)"

MATERIALS
Tahki-Stacy Charles's *Jolie* (heavy worsted weight; 70% French angora/30% merino wool; each approx .87 oz/25 g and 108 yd/100 m), 12 (13, 14, 15, 16, 17) balls #5018 Salmon

Crochet hook, size G/6 (4.00 mm) or size needed to obtain gauge

To decrease 2 sts each side, ch 2 to turn; skip first st, (work a dec hdc to combine next 2 sts) twice; hdc into each st across until 5 sts rem, ending row with (dec hdc to combine next 2 sts) twice, hdc into top of turning-ch-2. Ch 2, turn.

Decrease half double crochet = dec hdc = Yarn over hook, insert hook into next st and pull up a loop (3 loops are on your hook); yarn over hook, insert hook into next st and pull up a loop; yarn over hook and draw loop through all 5 loops on hook.

For sweater assembly, refer to the illustration for set-in construction on page 126.

Next Row (RS): Skip first hdc, hdc into next 22 (25, 29, 33, 37, 41) sts, 2 hdc into next st, hdc into next 27 sts, 2 hdc into next st, hdc into each st across to end row—77 (83, 91, 99, 107, 115) sts.

Cont even in patt as established until piece measures approx 13" from beg, ending after WS row. *Do not ch 2.* Turn.

Shape Armholes
Next Row (RS): Slip st into first 6 (6, 8, 9, 10, 14) sts, ch 2. Skip st where last slip st was worked, hdc into next st and into each st across until 5 (5, 7, 8, 9, 13) sts rem in row—67 (73, 77, 83, 89, 89) sts. Ch 2, turn, leaving rest of row unworked.

Dec 1 st each side every row 5 (7, 8, 10, 13, 13) times, then every other row 1 (1, 1, 1, 0, 0) times—55 (57, 59, 61, 63, 63) sts rem.

Cont even in patt as established until piece measures approx 19 (19½, 20, 20½, 21, 21)" from beg, ending after WS row. Ch 2, turn.

Shape Neck
Next Row (RS): Work across first 13 (14, 15, 16, 17, 17) sts, ch 2, turn, leaving rest of row unworked.

Dec 1 st at neck edge every row twice—11 (12, 13, 14, 15, 15) sts rem this side.

Cont even, if necessary, in patt as established until this side measures approx 20 (20½, 21, 21½, 22, 22)" from beg.

Fasten off.

For second side of neck, skip the middle 29 sts, and with RS facing, attach yarn with a slip st to next st and ch 2. Skip st where slip st was worked, and work across to end row.

Complete same as first side.

FRONT

Same as back until piece measures approx 16 (16½, 17, 17½, 18, 18)" from beg, ending after WS row. Ch 2, turn.

Shape Neck
Next Row (RS): Work across first 16 (17, 18, 19, 20, 20) sts, ch 2, turn, leaving rest of row unworked.

Dec 1 st at neck edge every row twice, then every other row 3 times—11 (12, 13, 14, 15, 15) sts rem this side.

Cont even, if necessary, in patt as established until this side measures approx 20 (20½, 21, 21½, 22, 22)" from beg.

Fasten off.

For second side of neck, with RS facing, skip the middle 23 sts, and attach yarn with a slip st to next st and ch 2. Skip st where slip st was worked, and work across to end row.

Complete same as first side.

SLEEVES

Ch 44 (44, 44, 48, 48, 48).

Beg Solid Hdc Patt, and inc 1 st each side every other row 4 (7, 8, 10, 13, 13) times, then every fourth row 5 (4, 4, 3, 2, 2) times—61 (65, 67, 73, 77, 77) sts.

Cont even in patt as established until piece measures approx 10¾ (11¼, 11¾, 12, 12¼, 12¼)" from beg, ending after WS row. *Do not ch 2.* Turn.

Shape Cap
Next Row (RS): Slip st into first 6 (6, 8, 9, 10, 14) sts, ch 2. Skip st where last slip st was worked, hdc into next st and into each st across until 5 (5, 7, 8, 9, 13) sts rem—51 (55, 53, 57, 59, 51) sts. Ch 2, turn, leaving rest of row unworked.

Cont even in patt as established for 0 (1, 1, 1, 1, 2) rows.

Dec 1 st each side every row 8 (12, 13, 15, 14, 16) times—35 (31, 27, 27, 31, 19) sts rem.

Dec 2 sts each side every row 4 (3, 2, 2, 3, 0) times—19 sts rem. *Do not ch 2.* Turn.

Next Row: Slip st into first 3 sts, ch 2. Skip st where last slip st was worked, hdc into next st and into each st across until 2 sts rem—15 sts. *Do not ch 2.* Turn.

Next Row: Slip st into first 3 sts, ch 2. Skip st where last slip st was worked, hdc into next st and into each st across until 2 sts rem—11 sts.

Fasten off.

FINISHING

Sew shoulder seams.

Neckline Edging

With RS facing, attach yarn with a slip st to left shoulder seam and ch 1.

Rnd 1 (RS): Work 76 sc evenly spaced around neckline. Join with a slip st to first sc.

Rnd 2: Ch 15, skip first 2 sc, *sc into next sc, ch 15, skip next sc. Repeat from * around, ending rnd with a slip st to first sc.

Rnd 3: Ch 15, skip first sc, *sc into next sc, ch 15, skip next sc. Repeat from * around, ending rnd with a slip st to first sc.

Fasten off.

Set in sleeves. Sew sleeve and side seams.

Sleeve Edging

With RS facing, attach yarn with a slip st to sleeve seam and ch 1.

Rnd 1 (RS): Working into unused loops of foundation chain, work 42 (42, 42, 46, 46, 46) sc around lower edge of sleeve. Join with a slip st to first sc.

Complete same as neck edging.

Lower Edging

With RS facing, attach yarn with a slip st to lower left side seam and ch 1.

Rnd 1 (RS): Working into unused loops of foundation chain, work 136 (148, 164, 180, 196, 212) sc around entire lower edge. Join with a slip st to first sc.

Complete same as neck edging.

COOL TIP For a clean, modern look, omit the ruffles and finish off all edgings after Round 1.

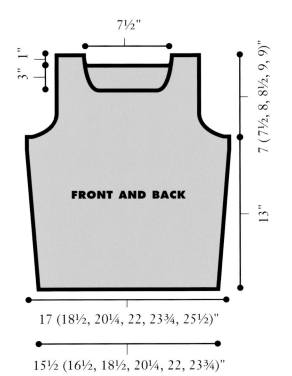

FRONT AND BACK

7½"

3"   1"

7 (7½, 8, 8½, 9, 9)"

13"

17 (18½, 20¼, 22, 23¾, 25½)"

15½ (16½, 18½, 20¼, 22, 23¾)"

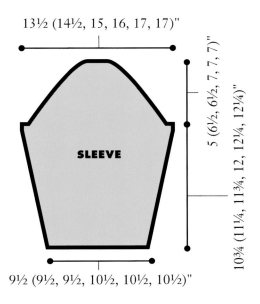

SLEEVE

13½ (14½, 15, 16, 17, 17)"

5 (6½, 6½, 7, 7, 7)"

10¾ (11¼, 11¾, 12, 12¼, 12¼)"

9½ (9½, 9½, 10½, 10½, 10½)"

Note: Measurements in schematic drawings do not include edging.

Francesca

It seems that everyone's wearing ponchos these days! With its silk and alpaca fabric and special beaded tassels, this one's particularly beautiful.

GAUGE

In Openwork Patt with larger hook, 7 dc = 1" wide and ½" high. To measure your gauge, make a test swatch as follows: Ch 38. Work Openwork Patt for 9 rows total. Fasten off. Piece should measure 5" wide and 4½" high. **To save time, take time to check gauge.**

OPENWORK PATTERN
(mult 14 + 7 sts)

Foundation Row (WS): Dc into sixth ch from hook, (ch 1, skip next ch, dc into next ch) twice, *ch 3, skip next 3 ch, sc into next ch, ch 3, skip next 3 ch, (dc into next ch, ch 1, skip next ch) 3 times, dc into next ch. Repeat from * across. Ch 3, turn.

Row 1 (RS): Skip first dc, (dc into next ch-1 sp, dc into next dc) 3 times, *ch 3, sc into next sc, ch 3, (dc into next dc, dc into next ch-1 sp) 3 times, dc into next dc. Repeat from * across, ending row with ch 3, sc into next sc, ch 3, (dc into next dc, dc into next ch-1 sp) twice, dc into next dc, dc under turning-ch, dc into third ch of turning-ch-4. Ch 4, turn.

Row 2: Skip first 2 dc, (dc into next dc, ch 1, skip next dc) twice, dc into next dc, *ch 3, sc into next sc, ch 3, (dc into next dc, ch 1, skip next dc) 3 times, dc into next dc. Repeat from * across, ending row with ch 3, sc into next sc, ch 3, (dc into next dc, ch 1, skip next dc) 3 times, dc into top of turning-ch-3. Ch 3, turn.

Continued on next page.

PONCHO

With larger hook, ch 318.

Beg Openwork Patt, and work even until piece measures approx 22" from beg, ending after Row 2 of patt. Ch 3, turn.

Shape Neck

Row 1 (RS): Skip first dc, (dc into next ch-1 sp, dc into next dc) 3 times, *ch 7, (dc into next dc, dc into next ch-1 sp) 3 times, dc into next dc. Repeat from * 7 more times. Ch 4, turn, leaving rest of row unworked.

Row 2: Skip first 2 dc, (dc into next dc, ch 1, skip next dc) twice, dc into next dc, *ch 3, skip next 3 ch, sc into next ch, ch 3, (dc into next dc, ch 1, skip next dc) 3 times, dc into next dc. Repeat from * 6 more times, ending row with ch 3, skip next 3 ch, sc into next ch, ch 3, (dc into next dc, ch 1, skip next dc) 3 times, dc into top of turning-ch-3. Ch 3, turn.

SKILL LEVEL
Advanced Beginner

SIZES
One size fits all

FINISHED MEASUREMENTS
Approx 45" wide and 22¾" long

MATERIALS
Blue Sky Alpaca's *Alpaca & Silk* (sport weight; 50% alpaca/ 50% silk; each approx 1¾ oz/ 50 g and 146 yd/133 m), 16 balls Spring #16

Crochet hooks, sizes D/3 and E/4 (3.25 and 3.50 mm) or size needed to obtain gauge

Seventy-two triangular glass beads (Blue Moon Beads's *Green Lined Yellow Tri Style #58485* was used on sample project.)

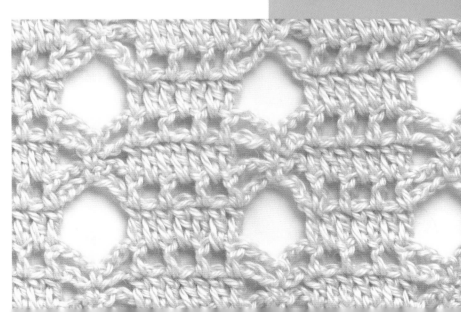

Row 3: Skip first dc, (dc into next ch-1 sp, dc into next dc) 3 times, *ch 7, (dc into next dc, dc into next ch-1 sp) 3 times, dc into next dc. Repeat from * across, ending row with ch 7, (dc into next dc, dc into next ch-1 sp) twice, dc into next dc, dc under turning-ch, dc into third ch of turning-ch-4. Ch 4, turn.

Row 4: Skip first 2 dc, (dc into next dc, ch 1, skip next dc) twice, dc into next dc, *ch 3, skip next 3 ch, sc into next ch, ch 3, (dc into next dc, ch 1, skip next dc) 3 times, dc into next dc. Repeat from * across, ending row with ch 3, skip next 3 ch, sc into next ch, ch 3, (dc into next dc, ch 1, skip next dc) 3 times, dc into top of turning-ch-3. Ch 3, turn.

Repeat Rows 1-4 for patt.

NOTES

Constructionwise, this poncho is made in one piece, up the front, over the shoulders, and down the back.

Throughout, each dc, sc, and ch-1 sp counts as 1 st.

Bead ch = Move a bead up next to the hook, yarn over hook and draw loop through the loop on the hook, locking bead into the st.

Row 3: Skip first dc, (dc into next ch-1 sp, dc into next dc) 3 times, *ch 3, sc into next sc, ch 3, (dc into next dc, dc into next ch-1 sp) 3 times, dc into next dc. Repeat from * across, ending row with ch 3, sc into next sc, ch 3, (dc into next dc, dc into next ch-1 sp) twice, dc into next dc, dc under turning-ch, dc into third ch of turning-ch-4. Ch 4, turn.

Row 4: Skip first 2 dc, (dc into next dc, ch 1, skip next dc) twice, dc into next dc, *ch 3, sc into next sc, ch 3, (dc into next dc, ch 1, skip next dc) 3 times, dc into next dc. Repeat from * across, ending row with ch 3, sc into next sc, ch 3, (dc into next dc, ch 1, skip next dc) 3 times, dc into top of turning-ch-3. Ch 3, turn.

Remove hook from loop.

For second side of neck, with RS facing, skip the middle 77 sts and attach yarn with a slip st to next dc and ch 3, skip the st where slip st was worked, *(dc into next dc, dc into next ch-1 sp) 3 times, dc into next dc, ch 7. Repeat from * 7 more times, ending row with (dc into next dc, dc into next ch-1 sp) twice, dc into next dc, dc under turning-ch, dc into third ch of turning-ch-4. Ch 4, turn.

Work Neck Shaping Rows 2-4 on this side.

Fasten off.

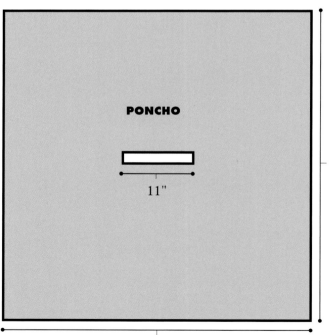

PONCHO

11"

45½"

45"

Joining after Neck Shaping

Skip first dc, (dc into next ch-1 sp, dc into next dc) 3 times, *ch 7, (dc into next dc, dc into next ch-1 sp) 3 times, dc into next dc. Repeat from * 7 more times; ch 77 for neck opening; skip the middle 77 sts; **(dc into next dc, dc into next ch-1 sp) 3 times, dc into next dc, ch 7. Repeat from ** 7 more times, (dc into next dc, dc into next ch-1 sp) twice, dc into next dc, dc under turning-ch, dc into third ch of turning-ch-4. Ch 4, turn.

Next Row: Skip first 2 dc, (dc into next dc, ch 1, skip next dc) twice, dc into next dc, *ch 3, skip next 3 ch, sc into next ch, ch 3, (dc into next dc, ch 1, skip next dc) 3 times, dc into next dc. Repeat from * 7 more times; **ch 3, skip next 3 ch, sc into next ch, ch 3, skip next 3 ch, (dc into next ch, ch 1, skip next ch) twice, dc into next ch. Repeat from ** 9 more times, ch 3, skip next 3 ch, sc into next ch, ch 3, skip next 3 ch; ***(dc into next dc, ch 1, skip next dc) twice, dc into next dc, ch 3, skip next 3 ch, sc into next ch, ch 3. Repeat from *** across, ending row with (dc into next dc, ch 1, skip next dc) twice, dc into top of turning-ch-3. Ch 3, turn.

Cont even in patt as established until piece measures approx 45½" from beg, ending after Row 2 of patt.

Fasten off.

FINISHING

Side Edging

With RS facing and smaller hook, work 275 sc evenly spaced along each side edge of poncho.

Fasten off.

Tassel Caps *(Make 4)*

Prethread 12 beads onto yarn.

With smaller hook, ch 2.

Rnd 1 (RS): 12 sc into second ch from hook. Do not join; work rest of piece in continuous rnds.

Rnds 2-7: Sc into each sc.

Rnd 8: *Sc into next sc, ch 1, bead ch, ch 1, slip st into top of last sc. Repeat from * around, ending rnd with a slip st to first sc.

Fasten off.

Tassels *(Make 4)*

Wrap yarn 68 times around a 6" piece of cardboard.

Cut strands along one end and tie them tightly tog at center, leaving an 8" tail.

Pull this yarn tail through the center of tassel cap. Thread 6 beads onto this tail, then attach tassel to corner of poncho. Trim evenly.

COOL TIP For a warmer garment, crochet your poncho out of a lofty mohair yarn. It'll still be lightweight but nice and cozy!

Laura

The pebbly texture of this sweet-looking shell comes from alternating single and double crochet stitches.

GAUGE

In Textured Patt with larger hook, 22 sts and 20 rows = 4". To measure your gauge, make a test swatch as follows: Ch 23. Work Textured Patt on 22 sts for 20 rows total. Fasten off. Piece should measure 4" square. **To save time, take time to check gauge.**

TEXTURED PATTERN

(mult 2 sts)

Foundation Row (RS): Sc into third ch from hook, *dc into next ch, sc into next ch. Repeat from * across, ending row with dc into next ch, hdc into last ch. Ch 2, turn.

Patt Row: Skip first hdc, *sc into next dc, dc into next sc. Repeat from * across, ending row with hdc into top of turning-ch-2. Ch 2, turn.

Repeat Patt Row for patt.

NOTES

Throughout, each sc, hdc, dc, dec hdc, and turning-ch-2 counts as 1 st.

To decrease 1 st each side, ch 2 to turn; skip first st, work a dec hdc to combine next 2 sts; cont across row until 3 sts rem, ending row with dec hdc to combine next 2 sts, hdc into top of turning-ch-2. Ch 2, turn.

Decrease half double crochet = dec hdc = Yarn over hook, insert hook into next st and pull up a loop (3 loops are on your hook); yarn over hook, insert hook into next st and pull up a loop; yarn over hook and draw loop through all 5 loops on hook.

BACK

With larger hook, ch 91 (101, 111, 121, 131, 141).

Beg Textured Patt, and work even on 90 (100, 110, 120, 130, 140) sts until piece measures approx 9½ (9½, 9½, 9½, 9½, 10)" from beg, ending after WS row.

Fasten off.

Shape Armholes

With RS facing, skip first 12 (12, 16, 16, 20, 20) sts, attach yarn with a slip st to next st and ch 2. Skip st where last slip st was worked, cont patt as established until 12 (12, 16, 16, 20, 20) sts rem in row. Ch 2, turn, leaving rest of row unworked—66 (76, 78, 88, 90, 100) sts rem.

Dec 1 st each side every row 6 (9, 9, 12, 12, 14) times—54 (58, 60, 64, 66, 72) sts rem.

Cont even in patt as established until piece measures approx 14½ (15, 15, 15½, 15½, 16½)" from beg, ending after WS row. Ch 2, turn.

Shape Neck

Next Row: Skip first st, work patt as established across next 11 (13, 14, 16, 17, 20) sts—12 (14, 15, 17, 18, 21) sts. Ch 2, turn, leaving rest of row unworked.

SKILL LEVEL
Intermediate

SIZES
Extra-Small (Small, Medium, Large, Extra-Large, Extra-Extra-Large). *Instructions are for smallest size, with changes for other sizes noted in parentheses as necessary.*

FINISHED MEASUREMENTS
Bust: 33 (36, 40, 44, 47½, 51)"
Total length (including edging): 16¾ (17¼, 17¼, 17¾, 17¾, 18¾)"

MATERIALS
Coats and Clark's *Lustersheen* (fingering weight; 100% acrylic; each approx 4 oz/ 113 g and 335 yd/306 m), 3 (3, 4, 4, 5, 6) skeins Turquoise #517
Crochet hooks, sizes D/3 and E/4 (3.25 and 3.50 mm) or size needed to obtain gauge

Dec 1 st at neck edge every row 5 times—7 (9, 10, 12, 13, 16) sts rem.

Cont even, if necessary, in patt as established until piece measures approx 16 (16½, 16½, 17, 17, 18)" from beg.

Fasten off.

For second side of neck, skip the middle 30 sts, and with RS facing, attach yarn with a slip st to next st and ch 2. Skip st where slip st was worked, work patt as established to end row.

Complete same as first side.

Fasten off.

FRONT

Same as back until piece measures approx 11¼ (11¾, 11¾, 12¼, 12¼, 13¼)" from beg, ending after RS row. Ch 2, turn.

Shape Neck
Next Row: Skip first st, work patt as established across next 17 (19, 20, 22, 23, 26) sts—18 (20, 21, 23, 24, 27) sts. Ch 2, turn, leaving rest of row unworked.

Dec 1 st at neck edge every row 5 times, then every other row 6 times—7 (9, 10, 12, 13, 16) sts rem.

Cont even in patt as established until this side measures same as back to shoulders.

Fasten off.

For second side of neck, skip the middle 18 sts, and with RS facing, attach yarn with a slip st to next st and ch 2. Skip st where slip st was worked, work patt as established to end row.

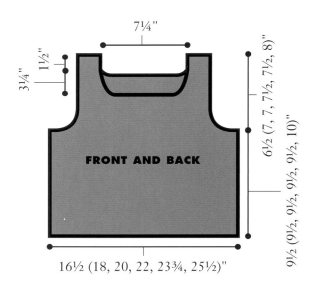

7¼"
1½"
3¼"
FRONT AND BACK
6½ (7, 7, 7½, 7½, 8)"
9½ (9½, 9½, 9½, 9½, 10)"
16½ (18, 20, 22, 23¾, 25½)"

Note: Measurements in schematic drawing do not include edging.

COOL TIP For a funkier look, omit the lower body edging and attach three strands of fringe to every other stitch all the way around the lower edge.

Complete same as first side.

Fasten off.

FINISHING
Lower Back Edging
With RS facing and smaller hook, attach yarn with a slip st to lower edge of back and ch 1.

Row 1 (RS): Working into unused loops of foundation chain, work 91 (101, 111, 121, 131, 141) sc evenly spaced along lower edge. Ch 1, turn.

Row 2: Sc into each sc across. Ch 1, turn.

Row 3: Sc into first sc, *ch 2, skip next 4 sc, (dc, ch 3, dc, ch 3, dc) into next sc, ch 2, skip next 4 sc, sc into next sc. Repeat from * across. Ch 1, turn.

Row 4: Sc into first sc, *5 dc into next ch-3 sp, ch 4, slip st into third ch from hook, ch 1, 5 dc into next ch-3 sp, sc into next sc. Repeat from * across.

Fasten off.

Lower Front Edging
With RS facing and smaller hook, attach yarn with a slip st to lower edge of front.

Complete same as lower back edging.

Sew shoulder seams.

Neckline Edging
With RS facing and smaller hook, attach yarn with a slip st to neck edge of right shoulder seam and ch 1.

Rnd 1 (RS): Work 130 sc evenly spaced around neckline. Join with a slip st to first sc.

Fasten off.

Sew side seams.

Armhole Edging
With RS facing and smaller hook, attach yarn with a slip st to upper side seam and ch 1.

Rnd 1 (RS): Work 93 (102, 102, 111, 111, 120) sc evenly spaced around armhole. Join with a slip st to first sc.

Fasten off.

Sherry

Decreases are cleverly hidden within the fabric of this A-line duster coat. Its strong vertical lines will flatter any figure!

GAUGE

In Wide Ribbed Shell Patt, 12 sts and 5 rows = 4". To measure your gauge, make a test swatch as follows: Ch 15. Work Wide Ribbed Shell Patt on 13 sts for 5 rows total. Fasten off. Piece should measure 4¼" wide and 4" high. **To save time, take time to check gauge.**

WIDE RIBBED SHELL PATTERN

(mult 6 + 1 sts)

Foundation Row (RS): (2 dc, ch 1, 2 dc) into sixth ch from hook, *skip next 2 ch, dc into next ch, skip next 2 ch, (2 dc, ch 1, 2 dc) into next ch. Repeat from * across, ending row with skip next 2 ch, dc into last ch. Ch 3, turn.

Row 1 (WS): Skip first 3 dc, *(2 dc, ch 1, 2 dc) into next ch-1 sp, skip next 2 dc, BPDC into next st, skip next 2 dc. Repeat from * across, ending row with (2 dc, ch 1, 2 dc) into next ch-1 sp, skip next 2 dc, dc into top of turning-ch-3. Ch 3, turn.

Row 2: Skip first 3 dc, *(2 dc, ch 1, 2 dc) into next ch-1 sp, skip next 2 dc, FPDC into next st, skip next 2 dc. Repeat from * across, ending row with (2 dc, ch 1, 2 dc) into next ch-1 sp, skip next 2 dc, dc into top of turning-ch-3. Ch 3, turn.

Repeat Rows 1 and 2 for patt.

MEDIUM RIBBED SHELL PATTERN

(mult 5 + 1 sts)

Row 1 (RS): Skip first 3 dc, *(2 dc, ch 1, dc) into next ch-1 sp, skip next 2 dc, FPDC into next st, skip next 2 dc. Repeat from * across, ending row with (2 dc, ch 1, dc) into next ch-1 sp, skip next 2 dc, dc into top of turning-ch-3. Ch 3, turn.

Continued on next page.

BACK

Ch 81 (93, 105, 117).

Beg Wide Ribbed Shell Patt, and work even on 79 (91, 103, 115) sts until piece measures approx 17" from beg, ending after WS row. Ch 3, turn.

Beg Medium Ribbed Shell Patt, and work even on 66 (76, 86, 96) sts until piece measures approx 34" from beg, ending after WS row. Ch 3, turn.

Beg Narrow Ribbed Shell Patt, and work even on 53 (61, 69, 77) sts until piece measures approx 36" from beg, ending after WS row. *Do not ch 3.* Turn.

Shape Armholes

Next Row (RS): Slip st into first 5 (9, 9, 13) sts, ch 3. Skip st where last slip st was worked, skip next dc, *(dc, ch 1, dc) into next ch-1 sp, skip next dc, FPDC into next st, skip next dc. Repeat from * across until 7 (7, 11, 15) sts rem, ending row with (dc, ch 1, dc) into next ch-1 sp, skip next dc, dc into next st. Ch 3, turn, leaving rest of row unworked.

Cont even on 45 (45, 53, 53) sts in Narrow Ribbed Shell Patt as established until piece measures approx 45 (45, 45½, 45½)" from beg. Fasten off.

SKILL LEVEL
Intermediate

SIZES
Small (Medium, Large, Extra-Large). *Instructions are for smallest size, with changes for other sizes noted in parentheses as necessary.*

FINISHED MEASUREMENTS
Bust (buttoned): 34½ (39½, 45, 50½)"

Total length: 45 (45, 46½, 46½)"

MATERIALS
Aurora Yarns/Garnstudio's *Highlander* (bulky weight; 90% wool/10% nylon; each approx 1¾ oz/50 g and 87 yd/80 m), 23 (25, 27, 29) balls #04 Spring Moss

Crochet hook, size K/10.5 (6.50 mm) or size needed to obtain gauge

Eight (eight, nine, nine) ⅞" buttons (JHB International's *Castille Style #86598* was used on sample garment)

Row 2 (WS): Skip first 2 dc, *(2 dc, ch 1, dc) into next ch-1 sp, skip next 2 dc, BPDC into next st, skip next dc. Repeat from * across, ending row with (2 dc, ch 1, dc) into next ch-1 sp, skip next 2 dc, dc into top of turning-ch-3. Ch 3, turn.

Row 3: Skip first 2 dc, *(2 dc, ch 1, dc) into next ch-1 sp, skip next 2 dc, FPDC into next st, skip next dc. Repeat from * across, ending row with (2 dc, ch 1, dc) into next ch-1 sp, skip next 2 dc, dc into top of turning-ch-3. Ch 3, turn.

Repeat Rows 2 and 3 for patt.

NARROW RIBBED SHELL PATTERN
(mult 4 + 1 sts)

Row 1 (RS): Skip first 2 dc, *(dc, ch 1, dc) into next ch-1 sp, skip next 2 dc, FPDC into next st, skip next dc. Repeat from * across, ending row with (dc, ch 1, dc) into next ch-1 sp, skip next 2 dc, dc into top of turning-ch-3. Ch 3, turn.

Row 2 (WS): Skip first 2 dc, *(dc, ch 1, dc) into next ch-1 sp, skip next dc, BPDC into next st, skip next dc. Repeat from * across, ending row with (dc, ch 1, dc) into next ch-1 sp, skip next dc, dc into top of turning-ch-3. Ch 3, turn.

Row 3: Skip first 2 dc, *(dc, ch 1, dc) into next ch-1 sp, skip next dc, FPDC into next st, skip next dc. Repeat from * across, ending row with (dc, ch 1, dc) into next ch-1 sp, skip next dc, dc into top of turning-ch-3. Ch 3, turn.

Repeat Rows 2 and 3 for patt.

NOTES

Throughout, each dc, ch-1 sp, BPDC, FPDC, and turning-ch-3 counts as 1 st.

BPDC = Yarn over hook, insert hook *from back to front to back* around the post of indicated stitch, yarn over hook and pull up a loop; (yarn over hook and draw loop through 2 loops on hook) twice. Unless noted otherwise, always skip the st behind the BPDC.

FPDC = Yarn over hook, insert hook *from front to back to front* around the post of indicated stitch, yarn over hook and pull up a loop; (yarn over hook and draw loop through 2 loops on hook) twice. Unless noted otherwise, always skip the st behind the FPDC.

When sewing sleeve seams, be sure to reverse the lower 3½" of sleeve seam so it will be hidden when the cuff is folded back.

For sweater assembly, refer to the illustration for square indented construction on page 126.

LEFT FRONT

Ch 39 (45, 51, 57).

Beg Wide Ribbed Shell Patt, and work even on 37 (43, 49, 55) sts until piece measures approx 17" from beg, ending after WS row. Ch 3, turn.

Beg Medium Ribbed Shell Patt, and work even on 31 (36, 41, 46) sts until piece measures approx 34" from beg, ending after WS row. Ch 3, turn.

Beg Narrow Ribbed Shell Patt, and work even on 25 (29, 33, 37) sts until piece measures approx 36" from beg, ending after WS row. *Do not ch 3.* Turn.

Shape Armhole
Next Row (RS): Slip st into first 5 (9, 9, 13) sts, ch 3. Skip st where last slip st was worked, skip next dc, *(dc, ch 1, dc) into next ch-1 sp, skip next dc, FPDC into next st, skip next dc. Repeat from * across, ending row with (dc, ch 1, dc) into next ch-1 sp, skip next dc, dc into top of turning-ch-3. Ch 3, turn.

Cont even on 21 (21, 25, 25) sts in patt as established until piece measures approx 42 (42, 42½, 42½)" from beg, ending after RS row. *Do not ch 3.* Turn.

Shape Neck
Next Row (WS): Slip st into first 5 sts, ch 3. Skip st where last slip st was worked, skip next dc, *(dc, ch 1, dc) into next ch-1 sp, skip next dc, BPDC into next st, skip next dc. Repeat from * across, ending row with *(dc, ch 1, dc) into next ch-1 sp, skip next dc, dc into top of turning-ch-3. Ch 3, turn.

Next Row: Work patt as established until 4 sts rem in row, ending row with hdc into last ch-1 sp. Ch 3, turn.

Cont even on 13 (13, 17, 17) sts in Narrow Ribbed Shell Patt as established until piece measures same as back to shoulders. Fasten off.

RIGHT FRONT

Same as left front until piece measures same as left front to armhole, ending after WS row. Ch 3, turn.

Shape Armhole
Next Row (RS): Work patt as established until 4 sts rem in row. Ch 3, turn, leaving rest of row unworked— 21 (21, 25, 25) sts.

Cont even in Narrow Ribbed Shell Patt as established until piece measures same as left front to neck shaping, ending after RS row. Ch 3, turn.

Shape Neck
Next Row (WS): Work patt as established until 5 sts rem, ending row with dc into top of next st. *Do not ch 3.* Turn.

Next Row: Slip st into first 5 sts, ch 3, skip st where last slip st was worked, skip next dc, *(dc, ch 1, dc) into next ch-1 sp, skip next dc, FPDC into next st, skip next dc. Repeat from * across, ending row with (dc, ch 1, dc) into next ch-1 sp, skip next dc, dc into top of turning-ch-3. Ch 3, turn.

Complete same as left front.

SLEEVES

Ch 39 (39, 43, 43).

Foundation Row (RS): (Dc, ch 1, dc) into fifth ch from hook, *skip next ch, dc into next ch, skip next ch, (dc, ch 1, dc) into next ch. Repeat from * across, ending row with skip next ch, dc into last ch. Ch 3, turn.

Cont even on 37 (37, 41, 41) sts in Narrow Ribbed Shell Patt as established until piece measures approx 7" from beg, ending after WS row. Ch 3, turn.

Increase Row 1 (RS): Dc into first dc, *(dc, ch 1, dc) into next ch-1 sp, skip next dc, FPDC into next st, skip next dc. Repeat from * across, ending row with (dc, ch 1, dc) into next ch-1 sp, skip next dc, 2 dc into top of turning-ch-3. Ch 4, turn.

Increase Row 2: Dc into first dc, dc into next dc, *(dc, ch 1, dc) into next ch-1 sp, skip next dc, BPDC into next st, skip next dc. Repeat from * across, ending row with (dc, ch 1, dc) into next ch-1 sp, skip next dc, dc into next dc, (dc, ch 1, dc) into top of turning-ch-3. Ch 3, turn.

Increase Row 3: Skip first dc, *(dc, ch 1, dc) into next ch-1 sp, skip next dc, FPDC into next st, skip next dc. Repeat from * across, ending row with (dc, ch 1, dc) under turning-ch-4, dc into third ch of turning-ch-4. Ch 3, turn.

Increase Row 4: Skip first 2 dc, *(dc, ch 1, dc) into next ch-1 sp, skip next dc, BPDC into next st, skip next dc. Repeat from * across, ending row with (dc, ch 1, dc) into next ch-1 sp, skip next dc, dc into top of turning-ch-3. Ch 3, turn.

Cont even in Narrow Ribbed Shell Patt as established for 14 (14, 14, 12) rows. Ch 3, turn.

Repeat Sleeve Increase Rows 1-4 once more— 53 (53, 57, 57) sts. Ch 3, turn.

Cont even in Narrow Ribbed Shell Patt as established until piece measures approx 24½ (24½, 23½, 23½)" from beg. Fasten off.

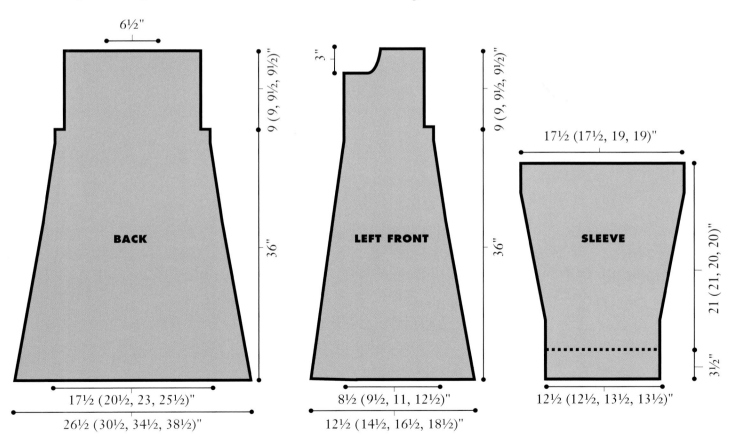

Note: Measurements in schematic drawings do not include lower edging.

FINISHING

Sew 13 (13, 17, 17) sts tog for each shoulder seam.

Collar

Ch 59.

Foundation Row (RS): (Dc, ch 1, dc) into fifth ch from hook, *skip next ch, dc into next ch, skip next ch, (dc, ch 1, dc) into next ch. Repeat from * across, ending row with skip next ch, dc into last ch—57 sts. Ch 3, turn.

Next Row: Skip first 2 dc, *(2 dc, ch 1, dc) into next ch-1 sp, skip next dc, BPDC into next st, skip next dc. Repeat from * across, ending row with (2 dc, ch 1, dc) into next ch-1 sp, skip next dc, dc into top of turning-ch-3—71 sts. Ch 3, turn.

Next Row: Skip first 2 dc, *(2 dc, ch 1, dc) into next ch-1 sp, skip next 2 dc, FPDC into next st, skip next dc. Repeat from * across, ending row with (2 dc, ch 1, dc) into next ch-1 sp, skip next 2 dc, dc into top of turning-ch-3. Ch 3, turn.

Next Row: Skip first 2 dc, *(2 dc, ch 1, 2 dc) into next ch-1 sp, skip next 2 dc, BPDC into next st, skip next dc. Repeat from * across, ending row with (2 dc, ch 1, 2 dc) into next ch-1 sp, skip next 2 dc, dc into top of turning-ch-3—85 sts. Ch 3, turn.

Next Row: Skip first 2 dc, *(2 dc, ch 1, 2 dc) into next ch-1 sp, skip next 2 dc, FPDC into next st, skip next 2 dc. Repeat from * across, ending row with (2 dc, ch 1, 2 dc) into next ch-1 sp, skip next 2 dc, dc into top of turning-ch-3. Fasten off.

Front Edging

With RS facing, attach yarn with a slip st to lower right front edge and ch 1. Work 1 row of sc evenly spaced along right front edge, around back of neck, and down left front edge, working 3 sc at beg of each front neck shaping. Ch 1, turn. Place markers for 8 (8, 9, 9) evenly spaced buttons on left front edge, making the first ½" from beg of neck shaping and the last 10" from lower edge.

Next Row: Cont in sc, working 3 sc at beg of each front neck shaping, and making buttonholes on right front by working (ch 2, skip next 2 sc) opposite markers.

Next Row: Cont in sc, working 3 sc at beg of each front neck shaping, and working 2 sc into each ch-2 sp. Fasten off.

Lower Edging

With RS facing, attach yarn with a slip st to lower left front edge and ch 1. Working into unused loops of foundation chain, work sc evenly spaced around entire lower edge. Fasten off.

Sew on collar.

Collar Edging

With RS of collar facing, attach yarn with a slip st to lower edge of collar, and ch 1. Work 1 row of sc evenly spaced around entire edge of collar, working 3 sc into each corner. Fasten off.

Set in sleeves. Sew sleeve and side seams.

Sleeve Edging

With WS facing, attach yarn with a slip st to lower sleeve seam, and ch 1. Working into unused loops of foundation chain, work 1 row of sc evenly spaced around. Join with a slip st to first sc. Fasten off.

Sew on buttons.

COOL TIP Don't let those FPDCs and BPDCs confuse you! To make things easier, mark the right side of the fabric with a contrasting piece of yarn. Made correctly, all of those front- and back-post relief stitches will "pop out" onto the public side of the fabric.

Davida

From its funky fringe to its sassy tassels, this skirt is a winner. The subtle A-line silhouette is created simply by changing hook sizes as you go.

GAUGE

In Color Patt with largest hook, 17 sts = 5" and 10 rows = 4". To measure your gauge, make a test swatch as follows: With largest hook, ch 19.

Foundation Row 1: Dc into fourth ch from hook, *ch 1, skip next ch, dc into next 5 ch. Repeat from * across, ending row with ch 1, skip next ch, dc into last 2 ch. Change color, ch 3, turn.

Foundation Row 2: Skip first dc, dc into next dc, *long dc into corresponding ch of foundation ch, dc into next 2 dc, ch 1, skip next dc, dc into next 2 dc. Repeat from * across, ending row with long dc into corresponding ch of foundation ch, dc into next dc, dc into top of turning-ch-3. Change color, ch 3, turn.

Row 1: Skip first st, dc into next st, *ch 1, skip next st, dc into next 2 sts, long dc, dc into next 2 sts. Repeat from * across, ending row with ch 1, skip next st, dc into next st, dc into top of turning-ch-3. Change color, ch 3, turn.

Row 2: Skip first st, dc into next st, *long dc, dc into next 2 sts, ch 1, skip next st, dc into next 2 sts. Repeat from * across, ending row with long dc, dc into next st, dc into top of turning-ch-3. Change color, ch 3, turn.

Repeat Rows 1 and 2 in Color Sequence on 17 sts for 10 rows total. Fasten off.

Piece should measure 4" wide and 5" high. **To save time, take time to check gauge.**

Continued on next page.

SKIRT

With smallest hook and A, ch 132 (156, 180). Being careful not to twist chain, join with a slip st to form a ring. Ch 3.

Foundation Rnd: Dc into each ch around—132 (156, 180) sts. Ch 3. *Do not turn.*

Next Rnd: Skip first dc, dc into each dc around, ending rnd with a slip st to top of ch-3—132 (156, 180) sts. Ch 3. *Do not turn.*

Repeat last rnd until piece measures approx 2" from beg. Change to B, ch 3. *Do not turn.*

Work Foundation Rnd of Color Patt, then cont even in patt as established in Color Sequence until piece measures approx 7½" from beg.

Change to middle-sized hook, and cont even in patt as established until piece measures approx 13½" from beg.

Change to largest hook, and cont even in patt as established until piece measures approx 19½" from beg, ending after Rnd 1 of patt. Change color, ch 3. *Do not turn.*

Next Rnd (RS): Skip first st, dc into next st, *long dc, dc into next 5 sts.

SKILL LEVEL
Intermediate

SIZES
Small (Medium, Large).
Instructions are for smallest size, with changes for other sizes noted in parentheses as necessary.

FINISHED MEASUREMENTS
Hip: 33 (39, 45)"
Total length (excluding fringe): 19"

MATERIALS
Brown Sheep Company's *Naturespun Worsted* (worsted weight; 100% wool; each approx 3½ oz/100 g and 245 yd/224 m), 2 (2, 3) skeins *each* of Cherry Delight #108 (A), Husker Red #N44 (B), and Orange You Glad #N54 (C)

Crochet hooks, sizes G/6, H/8, and I/9 (4.00, 5.00, and 5.50 mm) or size needed to obtain gauge

Elastic, ¾" wide, cut to fit waist

COLOR PATTERN
(mult 6 sts)

Foundation Rnd (RS): Skip first st, dc into next 4 sts, *ch 1, skip next st, dc into next 5 sts. Repeat from * around, ending rnd with ch 1, skip next st, slip st to top of ch-3. Change color, ch 3. *Do not turn.*

Rnd 1(RS): Skip first st, dc into next st, *ch 1, skip next st, dc into next 2 sts, long dc, dc into next 2 sts. Repeat from * around, ending rnd with ch 1, skip next st, dc into next 2 sts, long dc, slip st to top of ch-3. Change color, ch 3. *Do not turn.*

Rnd 2: Skip first st, dc into next st, long dc, dc into next 2 sts, ch 1, skip next st, *dc into next 2 sts, long dc, dc into next 2 sts, ch 1, skip next st. Repeat from * around, ending rnd with a slip st to top of ch-3. Change color, ch 3. *Do not turn.*

Repeat Rnds 1 and 2 in Color Sequence for patt.

COLOR SEQUENCE

One row or rnd *each* of *B, C, A. Repeat from * for patt.

NOTES

Throughout, each dc and ch-3 counts as 1 st.

Since this skirt is worked in the round, RS always faces you.

Constructionwise, this skirt is made in one piece, from the top down.

To change color, work the last stitch of the first color until 2 loops remain on your hook, then yarn over hook with the new color and complete the stitch.

For ease in finishing, do not cut the yarn after each stripe; instead, carry it loosely up the WS of the fabric until it is needed again.

Long dc = Elongated double crochet stitch worked into the corresponding skipped stitch *two rows or rnds below,* pulling up the first loop until it is even with hook.

Repeat from * around, ending rnd with long dc, dc into next 3 sts, slip st to top of ch-3.

Fasten off.

FINISHING

Fold waistband in half to WS, insert elastic, and *loosely* whipstitch into place.

Tie
With C, ch 195.

Thread tie through center of waistband.

If desired, make a tassel for each end of tie. (See *"Making a Tassel on a Crocheted Chain"* on the facing page.)

Fringe
With RS facing, attach fringe to lower edge of skirt. Trim fringe evenly.

- Beg with a 6" tail, crochet a chain to your desired length. Fasten off, leaving a 6" tail.

- Cut a piece of cardboard to your desired tassel length.

- Wind the yarn *loosely* around the cardboard several times; cut across one end.

- Tightly tie one of the yarn tails from the crocheted chain at the center of the strands to attach them to the lower section of the chain, and secure it with a square knot (*see* **1**).

- Fold down the upper half of the tassel to cover the yarn used to attach the strands to the crocheted chain.

- Wrap the tassel approximately 1" from the top and fasten off (*see* **2**).

- Trim tassel evenly.

15 (18, 20½)"

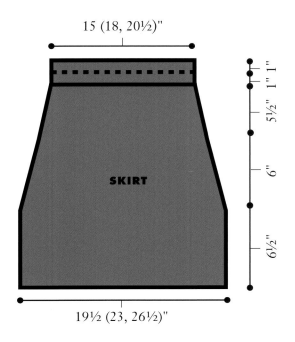

SKIRT

1" 1"

5½"

6"

6½"

19½ (23, 26½)"

Note: Skirt is made in the round; schematic drawing shows the measurements of skirt when laid flat; measurements in schematic drawing do not include fringe.

Giselle

Worn with or without its detachable scarf, this glittery number will take you from daytime into evening with style. And its lacy, flared cuffs are great fun to make!

GAUGE

In Textured Hdc Patt, with larger hook, 16 sts and 10 rows = 4". To measure your gauge, make a test swatch as follows: Ch 17. Work Textured Hdc Patt on 16 sts for 10 rows total. Fasten off. Piece should measure 4" square. **To save time, take time to check gauge.**

TEXTURED HALF DOUBLE CROCHET PATTERN

(mult 2 + 1 sts)

Foundation Row (RS): Hdc into third ch from hook and into each ch across. Ch 2, turn.

Patt Row: Skip first hdc, *hdc *into back loop only* of next st, hdc *into front loop only* of next st. Repeat from * across, ending row with hdc *into back loop only* of next st, hdc into top of turning-ch-2. Ch 2, turn.

Repeat Patt Row for patt.

NOTES

Throughout, each hdc and turning-ch-2 counts as 1 st.

Textured decrease = textured dec = Yarn over hook, insert hook into the appropriate loop of next st and pull up a loop (3 loops are on your hook); yarn over hook, insert hook into the appropriate loop of next st and pull up a loop; yarn over hook and draw loop through all 5 loops on hook.

To make a textured increase, work 2 hdc into 1 st, working 1 st *each* into the appropriate loops.

Continued on next page.

BACK

With larger hook, ch 72 (84, 96, 108, 120).

Beg Textured Hdc Patt, and work even on 71 (83, 95, 107, 119) sts until piece measures approx 3¼" from beg, ending after WS row. Ch 2, turn.

Shape Body

Decrease Row 1 (RS): Cont patt as established across first 20 (26, 32, 38, 44) sts, work a textured dec to combine the next 2 sts, cont patt as established over the middle 27 sts, work a textured dec to combine the next 2 sts, cont patt as established to end row—69 (81, 93, 105, 117) sts. Ch 2, turn.

Decrease Row 2: Work even in patt as established—69 (81, 93, 105, 117) sts. Ch 2, turn.

Decrease Row 3: Cont patt as established across first 20 (26, 32, 38, 44) sts, work a textured dec to combine the next 2 sts, cont patt as established over the middle 25 sts, work a textured dec to combine the next 2 sts, cont patt as established to end row—67 (79, 91, 103, 115) sts. Ch 2, turn.

SKILL LEVEL
Advanced

SIZES
Small (Medium, Large, Extra-Large, Extra-Extra-Large). *Instructions are for smallest size, with changes for other sizes noted in parentheses as necessary.*

FINISHED MEASUREMENTS
Bust: 35½ (41½, 47½, 53½, 59½)"

Total length: 22½ (23, 23½, 23½, 24)"

MATERIALS
Lion Brand's *Glitterspun* (heavy worsted weight; 60% acrylic/27% Cupro/13% polyester; each approx 1¾ oz/50 g and 115 yd/105 m), 11 (12, 14, 15, 17) balls Ruby #113

Crochet hooks, sizes I/9 and J/10 (5.50 and 6.00 mm) or size needed to obtain gauge

To decrease 1 st each side, ch 2 to turn; skip first st, work a dec hdc to combine next 2 sts; cont patt as established until 3 sts rem, ending row with dec hdc to combine next 2 sts, hdc into top of turning-ch-2. Ch 2, turn.

To decrease 2 sts each side, ch 2 to turn; skip first st, (work a dec hdc to combine next 2 sts) twice; cont patt as established until 5 sts rem, ending row with (dec hdc to combine next 2 sts) twice, hdc into top of turning-ch-2. Ch 2, turn.

Decrease half double crochet = dec hdc = Yarn over hook, insert hook into next st and pull up a loop (3 loops are on your hook); yarn over hook, insert hook into next st and pull up a loop; yarn over hook and draw loop through all 5 loops on hook.

Decrease single crochet = dec sc = (Insert hook into next st and pull up a loop) twice, yarn over hook and draw loop through all 3 loops on hook.

For sweater assembly, refer to the illustration for set-in construction on page 126.

Decrease Row 4: Work even in patt as established—67 (79, 91, 103, 115) sts. Ch 2, turn.

Decrease Row 5: Cont patt as established across first 20 (26, 32, 38, 44) sts, work a textured dec to combine the next 2 sts, cont patt as established over the middle 23 sts, work a textured dec to combine the next 2 sts, cont patt as established to end row—65 (77, 89, 101, 113) sts. Ch 2, turn.

Decrease Row 6: Work even in patt as established—65 (77, 89, 101, 113) sts. Ch 2, turn.

Decrease Row 7: Cont patt as established across first 20 (26, 32, 38, 44) sts, work a textured dec to combine the next 2 sts, cont patt as established over the middle 21 sts, work a textured dec to combine the next 2 sts, cont patt as established to end row—63 (75, 87, 99, 111) sts. Ch 2, turn.

Decrease Row 8: Work even in patt as established—63 (75, 87, 99, 111) sts. Ch 2, turn.

Decrease Row 9: Cont patt as established across first 20 (26, 32, 38, 44) sts, work a textured dec to combine the next 2 sts, cont patt as established over the middle 19 sts, work a textured dec to combine the next 2 sts, cont patt as established to end row—61 (73, 85, 97, 109) sts. Ch 2, turn.

Decrease Row 10: Work even in patt as established—61 (73, 85, 97, 109) sts. Ch 2, turn.

Decrease Row 11: Cont patt as established across first 20 (26, 32, 38, 44) sts, work a textured dec to combine the next 2 sts, cont patt as established over the middle 17 sts, work a textured dec to combine the next 2 sts, cont patt as established to end row—59 (71, 83, 95, 107) sts. Ch 2, turn.

Cont even in patt as established until piece measures approx 9½ (9½, 10, 10, 10)" from beg, ending after WS row. Ch 2, turn.

Increase Row 1 (RS): Cont patt as established across first 20 (26, 32, 38, 44) sts, work a textured inc into next st, cont patt as established over the middle 17 sts, work a textured inc into next st, cont patt as established to end row—61 (73, 85, 97, 109) sts. Ch 2, turn.

Increase Row 2: Work even in patt as established—61 (73, 85, 97, 109) sts. Ch 2, turn.

Increase Row 3: Cont patt as established across first 20 (26, 32, 38, 44) sts, work a textured inc into next st, cont patt as established over the middle 19 sts, work a textured inc into next st, cont patt as established to end row—63 (75, 87, 99, 111) sts. Ch 2, turn.

Increase Row 4: Work even in patt as established— 63 (75, 87, 99, 111) sts. Ch 2, turn.

Increase Row 5: Cont patt as established across first 20 (26, 32, 38, 44) sts, work a textured inc into next st, cont patt as established over the middle 21 sts, work a textured inc into next st, cont patt as established to end row—65 (77, 89, 101, 113) sts. Ch 2, turn.

Increase Row 6: Work even in patt as established— 65 (77, 89, 101, 113) sts. Ch 2, turn.

Increase Row 7: Cont patt as established across first 20 (26, 32, 38, 44) sts, work a textured inc into next st, cont patt as established over the middle 23 sts, work a textured inc into next st, cont patt as established to end row—67 (79, 91, 103, 115) sts. Ch 2, turn.

Increase Row 8: Work even in patt as established— 67 (79, 91, 103, 115) sts. Ch 2, turn.

Increase Row 9: Cont patt as established across first 20 (26, 32, 38, 44) sts, work a textured inc into next st, cont patt as established over the middle 25 sts, work a textured inc into next st, cont patt as established to end row—69 (81, 93, 105, 117) sts. Ch 2, turn.

Increase Row 10: Work even in patt as established— 69 (81, 93, 105, 117) sts. Ch 2, turn.

Increase Row 11: Cont patt as established across first 20 (26, 32, 38, 44) sts, work a textured inc into next st, cont patt as established over the middle 27 sts, work a textured inc into next st, cont patt as established to end row—71 (83, 95, 107, 119) sts. Ch 2, turn.

Cont even in patt as established until piece measures approx 15" from beg, ending after WS row. *Do not ch 3.* Turn.

Shape Armholes

Next Row (RS): Slip st into first 3 (6, 8, 11, 13) sts, ch 2, skip st where last slip st was worked, cont patt as established until 2 (5, 7, 10, 12) sts rem in row. Ch 2, turn, leaving rest of row unworked—67 (73, 81, 87, 95) sts.

Cont patt as established, and dec 2 sts each side every row 2 (3, 5, 7, 8) times, then dec 1 st each side every row 3 (4, 3, 2, 3) times—53 (53, 55, 55, 57) sts rem.

Cont even in patt as established until piece measures approx 21½ (22, 22½, 22½, 23)" from beg, ending after WS row. Ch 2, turn.

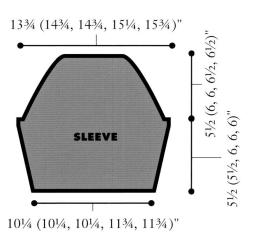

Note: Measurements in schematic drawings do not include sleeve edging.

Shape Neck

Work patt as established across first 13 (13, 14, 14, 15) sts. Ch 2, turn, leaving rest of row unworked.

Cont patt as established, and dec 1 st at neck edge once—12 (12, 13, 13, 14) sts rem. Ch 2, turn.

Cont even in patt as established until this side measures approx 22½ (23, 23½, 23½, 24)" from beg.

Fasten off.

For second side of neck, with RS facing, skip the middle 29 sts, and attach yarn with a slip st to next st and ch 2.

Complete same as first side.

FRONT

Same as back until piece measures approx 16 (16½, 17, 17, 17½)" from beg, ending after WS row. Ch 2, turn.

Place a marker on the middle st.

Shape Neck

Next Row (RS): Cont armhole shaping same as for back, *and at the same time,* work patt as established until 3 sts before marked st, work a dec hdc to combine the next 2 sts, hdc into next st. Ch 2, turn, leaving rest of row unworked.

Cont armhole shaping same as for back, *and at the same time,* dec 1 st at neck edge (as you did in the last row) every row 12 more times, then every other row once—12 (12, 13, 13, 14) sts rem this side.

Cont even in patt as established until this side measures same as back.

Fasten off.

For second side of neck, with RS facing, skip the middle st, and attach yarn with a slip st to next st and ch 2.

Complete same as first side.

SLEEVES

With larger hook, ch 42 (42, 42, 49, 49).

Beg Textured Hdc Patt on 41 (41, 41, 47, 47) sts, and inc 1 st each side every row 3 (7, 6, 2, 4) times, then every other row 4 (2, 3, 5, 4) times—55 (59, 59, 61, 63) sts.

Cont even in patt as established until piece measures approx 5½ (5½, 6, 6, 6)" from beg, ending after WS row. *Do not ch 2.* Turn.

Shape Cap

Next Row (RS): Slip st into first 3 (6, 8, 11, 13) sts, ch 2, skip st where last slip st was worked, cont patt as established until 2 (5, 7, 10, 12) sts rem. Ch 2, turn, leaving rest of row unworked.

Next Row: Work even in patt as established—51 (49, 45, 41, 39) sts rem. Ch 2, turn.

Cont patt as established, and dec 2 sts each side every row 3 (1, 0, 0, 0) times, dec 1 st each side every row 7 (10, 9, 4, 2) times, then dec 1 st each side every other row 0 (0, 1, 4, 5) times—25 sts rem. *Do not ch 2.* Turn.

Next Row: Slip st into first 3 sts, and ch 2. Skip st where last slip st was worked, hdc into each st across until 2 sts rem—21 sts.

Next Row: Slip st into first 3 sts, and ch 2. Skip st where last slip st was worked, hdc into each st across until 2 sts rem—17 sts.

Fasten off.

FINISHING

Sew shoulder seams.

Neckline Edging

With RS facing and smaller hook, attach yarn with a slip st to left shoulder seam and ch 1.

Rnd 1 (RS): Work 89 sc evenly spaced around neckline, working a dec sc at beg of front neck shaping and at beg of each back neck shaping. Join with a slip st to first sc.

Fasten off.

Set in sleeves. Sew side and sleeve seams.

Sleeve Edging

With RS facing and smaller hook, attach yarn with a slip st to lower sleeve seam and ch 1.

Rnd 1 (RS): Working into unused loops of foundation chain, work 42 (42, 42, 48, 48) sc evenly spaced around lower edge of sleeve. Join with a slip st to first sc. Ch 1.

Rnd 2: Sc into same st as slip st, sc into next sc, *ch 5, skip next 3 sc, sc into next 3 sc. Repeat from * around, ending rnd with ch 5, skip next 3 sc, sc into next sc. Join with a slip st to first sc. Ch 1.

Rnd 3: Sc into same st as slip st, *ch 3, sc into next ch-5 sp, ch 3, skip next sc, sc into next sc. Repeat from * around, ending rnd with ch 3, sc into next ch-5 sp, ch 3. Join with a slip st to first sc. Ch 5.

Rnd 4: Sc into first ch-3 sp, *sc into next sc, sc into next ch-3 sp, ch 5, sc into next ch-3 sp. Repeat from * around, ending rnd with sc into next sc, sc into next ch-3 sp, ch 2. Join with a slip st to third ch of beg ch-5. Ch 1.

Rnd 5: Sc into same st as slip st, *ch 3, skip next sc, sc into next sc, ch 3, sc into next ch-5 sp. Repeat from * around, ending rnd with ch 3, skip next sc, sc into next sc, ch 3. Join with a slip st to first sc. Ch 1.

Rnd 6: Sc into same st as slip st, *sc into next ch-3 sp, ch 7, sc into next ch-3 sp, sc into next sc. Repeat from * around, ending rnd with sc into next ch-3 sp, ch 7, sc into next ch-3 sp. Join with a slip st to first sc. Ch 1.

Rnd 7: Sc into same st as slip st, *ch 3, 3 sc into next ch-7 sp, ch 3, skip next sc, sc into next sc. Repeat from * around, ending rnd with ch 3, 3 sc into next ch-7 sp, ch 3. Join with a slip st to first sc. Ch 5.

Rnd 8: *Sc into next ch-3 sp, sc into next 3 sc, sc into next ch-3 sp, ch 7. Repeat from * around, ending rnd with sc into next ch-3 sp, sc into next 3 sc, sc into next ch-3 sp, ch 3. Join with a slip st to third ch of beg ch-5. Ch 1.

Rnd 9: Sc into same st as slip st, sc into next ch-3 sp, ch 3, *skip next sc, sc into next 3 sc, ch 3, 3 sc into next ch-7 sp, ch 3. Repeat from * around, ending rnd with skip next sc, sc into next 3 sc, ch 3, sc into next ch-3 sp. Join with a slip st to first sc. Ch 1.

Rnd 10: Sc into same st as slip st, sc into next sc, *sc into next ch-3 sp, ch 7, sc into next ch-3 sp, sc into next 3 sc. Repeat from * around, ending rnd with sc into next ch-3 sp, ch 7, sc into next ch-3 sp, sc into next sc. Join with a slip st to first sc. Ch 1.

Rnd 11: Sc into same st as slip st, sc into next sc, *ch 3, 3 sc into next ch-7 sp, ch 3, skip next sc, sc into next 3 sc. Repeat from * around, ending rnd with ch 3, 3 sc into next ch-7 sp, ch 3, skip next sc, sc into next sc. Join with a slip st to first sc. Ch 5.

Rnds 12 and 13: Same as Rnds 8 and 9.

Rnd 14: Sc into same st as slip st, sc into next sc, *3 sc into next ch-3 sp, sc into next 3 sc. Repeat from * around, ending rnd with 3 sc into next ch-3 sp, sc into next sc. Join with a slip st to first sc.

Fasten off.

Scarf
With larger hook, ch 22.

Foundation Row (RS): Sc into second ch from hook and into next 2 ch, *ch 7, skip next 5 ch, sc into next 5 ch. Repeat from * across, ending row with ch 7, skip next 5 ch, sc into next 3 ch. Ch 1, turn.

Row 1 (WS): Sc into first 2 sc, *ch 3, 3 sc into next ch-7 sp, ch 3, skip next sc, sc into next 3 sc. Repeat from * across, ending row with ch 3, 3 sc into next ch-7 sp, ch 3, skip next sc, sc into next 2 sc. Ch 6, turn.

Row 2: *Sc into ch-3 sp, sc into next 3 sc, sc into next ch-3 sp, ch 7. Repeat from * across, ending row with sc into ch-3 sp, sc into next 3 sc, sc into next ch-3 sp, ch 3, dc into last sc. Ch 1, turn.

Row 3: Sc into first dc, sc into ch-3 sp, *ch 3, skip next sc, sc into next 3 sc, ch 3, 3 sc into next ch-7 sp. Repeat from * across, ending row with ch 3, skip next sc, sc into next 3 sc, ch 3, 2 sc under turning-ch-6. Ch 1, turn.

Row 4: Sc into first 2 sc, *sc into next ch-3 sp, ch 7, sc into next ch-3 sp, sc into next 3 sc. Repeat from * across, ending row with sc into next ch-3 sp, ch 7, sc into next ch-3 sp, sc into next 2 sc. Ch 1, turn.

Repeat Rows 1-4 for patt until piece measures approx 42" from beg, ending after Row 3 of patt.

Next Row: Sc into first 2 sc, *sc into next ch-3 sp, ch 4, sc into next ch-3 sp, sc into next 3 sc. Repeat from * across, ending row with sc into next ch-3 sp, ch 4, sc into next ch-3 sp, sc into next 2 sc.

Fasten off.

Scarf Loop
With larger hook, ch 20.

Fasten off.

Attach chain to center of neckline on WS.

Thread scarf through loop to secure it to sweater.

Tasha

Make this glittery necklace and you'll feel like a princess! Go slowly while making it since the wire is much less flexible than the yarns and threads you're probably accustomed to crocheting with.

GAUGE

In patt, 20 ch = 4". To measure your gauge, make a test swatch as follows: Ch 20. Piece should measure 4" wide. **To save time, take time to check gauge.**

NOTE

Bead ch = Move a bead up next to the hook, yarn over hook and draw loop through the loop on the hook, locking bead into the st.

NECKLACE

Strand *(Make 1 with each color bead)*
Prethread 20 beads of a single color onto wire.

Leaving a 6" tail, *ch 3, bead ch. Repeat from * 19 more times, ending with ch 3.

Leaving a 6" tail, fasten off.

FINISHING

Holding all 4 strands tog in your free hand, thread 1 silver spacer bead onto the 4 strands.

Thread 1 bead tip through its tiny thread hole (with its open clamshell facing away from the crocheted chains) onto all 4 strands.

Thread 1 crimp bead onto all 4 strands.

Move these jewelry findings as close as possible to the crocheted chains.

Using crimping tool, crimp the crimp bead.

Trim wire.

Tightly enclose the compressed crimp bead inside the hinged clamshell part of the bead tip.

Put 1 jump ring onto the open hook, then close the hook.

Put 1 piece of necklace clasp onto the open jump ring. Close the jump ring. *(See the illustration to the left.)*

Repeat for other side of necklace.

COOL TIP Feeling groovy? Make your necklace with linen or hemp and wooden beads for a retro-hippie look. Makes a great anklet too—just change the length!

SKILL LEVEL
Advanced Beginner

FINISHED MEASUREMENT
Approx 17" (including clasp)

MATERIALS
Artbeads's *Silver Wire* (28-gauge; half-hard sterling; each spool approx 1 oz/28.5 g; 111 ft/ 34 m), 1 spool

Artbeads's *Crystal Bicone* (6 mm), 20 *each* of Light Siam #5301SIALT-6, Rose #5301RO-6, Siam #5301SIA-6, and Fuchsia #5301FU-6

Crochet hook, size B/1 (2.25mm) or size needed to obtain gauge

Two silver spacer beads (3 mm)

Two silver crimp beads

Two silver clamp-on bead tips

Two silver jump rings

One silver toggle clasp

Crimping pliers

Wire cutter

Alyssa

This bright pink halter hugs every curve, thanks to a cotton-Lycra® blend yarn.

GAUGE

In Solid Hdc Patt, *unstretched*, 23 sts and 16 rows = 4". To measure your gauge, make a test swatch as follows: Ch 24. Work Solid Hdc Patt on 23 sts for 16 rows total. Fasten off. Piece should measure 4" square *unstretched*. **To save time, take time to check gauge.**

SOLID HALF DOUBLE CROCHET PATTERN

(any number of sts)

Foundation Row (RS): Hdc into third ch from hook and into each ch across. Ch 2, turn.

Patt Row: Skip first hdc, *hdc into next hdc. Repeat from * across, ending row with hdc into top of turning-ch-2. Ch 2, turn.

Repeat Patt Row for patt.

NOTES

For a better fit, this body-conscious garment has negative ease.

Throughout, each hdc, dec hdc, and turning-ch-2 counts as 1 st.

To decrease 1 st each side, ch 2 to turn; skip first st, work a dec hdc to combine next 2 sts; hdc into each st across until 3 sts rem, ending row with dec hdc to combine next 2 sts, hdc into top of turning-ch-2. Ch 2, turn.

Decrease half double crochet = dec hdc = Yarn over hook, insert hook into next st and pull up a loop (3 loops are on your hook); yarn over hook, insert hook into next st and pull up a loop; yarn over hook and draw loop through all 5 loops on hook.

BACK

Ch 86 (92, 98, 104, 110).

Beg Solid Hdc Patt, and work even on 85 (91, 97, 103, 109) sts until piece measures approx 8½ (8½, 9½, 10, 10½)" from beg, ending after WS row.

Fasten off.

FRONT

Same as back until piece measures approx 8½ (8½, 9½, 10, 10½)" from beg, ending after WS row. Ch 2, turn.

Shape Armholes

Dec 1 st each side every row 20 (26, 22, 28, 29) times, then every other row 3 (0, 3, 0, 0) times—39 (39, 47, 47, 51) sts rem.

Cont even in patt as established for 2 rows.

Fasten off.

FINISHING

Lower Back Edging

With RS facing, attach yarn with a slip st to lower edge of back and ch 1.

SKILL LEVEL
Advanced Beginner

SIZES
Small (Medium, Large, Extra-Large, Extra-Extra-Large). *Instructions are for smallest size, with changes for other sizes noted in parentheses as necessary.*

FINISHED MEASUREMENTS
Bust: 29½ (32, 34, 36, 38)"
Total length (including edging): 16 (16, 17½, 18, 18¾)"

MATERIALS
Cascade's *Fixation* (sport weight; 98.3% cotton/ 1.7% elastic; each approx 1¾ oz/50 g and 100 yd/ 91 m unstretched), 4 (4, 5, 5, 6) balls Hot Pink #6185

Crochet hook, size E/4 (3.50 mm) or size needed to obtain gauge

Row 1 (RS): Working into unused loops of foundation chain, work 85 (91, 97, 103, 109) sc along lower edge. Ch 3, turn.

Row 2: Skip first 3 sc, *5 dc into next sc, ch 1, skip next 5 sc. Repeat from * across, ending row with 5 dc into next sc, skip next 2 sc, dc into last sc. Ch 1, turn.

Row 3: Sc into first dc, *skip next 2 dc, 5 dc into next dc, sc into next ch-1 sp. Repeat from * across, ending row with skip next 2 dc, 5 dc into next dc, sc into top of turning-ch-3.

Fasten off.

Lower Front Edging

With RS facing, attach yarn with a slip st to lower edge of front.

Complete same as lower back edging.

Sew side seams.

Armhole Edging

With RS facing, attach yarn with a slip st to upper left side seam and ch 1.

Work 1 row of sc evenly spaced along left armhole edge, across top of back, and along right armhole edge.

Fasten off.

Tie

Ch 375.

Slip st into second ch from hook and into each ch across. Fasten off.

Fold 2 rows at top of front to WS and *loosely* whipstitch into place.

Thread tie through fold.

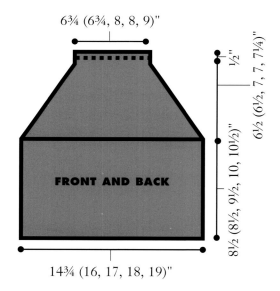

6¾ (6¾, 8, 8, 9)"

½"

6½ (6½, 7, 7, 7¼)"

FRONT AND BACK

8½ (8½, 9½, 10, 10½)"

14¾ (16, 17, 18, 19)"

Note: Measurements in schematic drawing do not include lower edging.

Katrina

Hats are all over New York's fashion runways—even in summertime! Here's a cool, cotton skully to keep you in style all year round.

GAUGE

Each motif measures 3½" square. To measure your gauge, make a test swatch as follows: Work Rnds 1-8 of motif. Fasten off. Piece should measure 3½" square. **To save time, take time to check gauge.**

MOTIF

With A, ch 2.

Rnd 1 (RS): 4 sc into second ch from hook. Join with a slip st to first sc. Ch 1.

Rnd 2: 3 sc into each sc around—12 sts. Join with a slip st to first sc. Change to B. Ch 1.

Rnd 3: Sc into same st as slip st, *3 sc into next sc, sc into next 2 sc. Repeat from * around, ending rnd with 3 sc into next sc, sc into next sc—20 sts. Join with a slip st to first sc. Ch 1.

Rnd 4: Sc into same st as slip st, sc into next sc, *3 sc into next sc, sc into next 4 sc. Repeat from * around, ending rnd with 3 sc into next sc, sc into next 2 sc—28 sts. Join with a slip st to first sc. Change to C. Ch 1.

Rnd 5: Sc into same st as slip st, sc into next 2 sc, *3 sc into next sc, sc into next 6 sc. Repeat from * around, ending rnd with 3 sc into next sc, sc into next 3 sc—36 sts. Join with a slip st to first sc. Ch 1.

Rnd 6: Sc into same st as slip st, sc into next 3 sc, *3 sc into next sc, sc into next 8 sc. Repeat from * around, ending rnd with 3 sc into next sc, sc into next 4 sc—44 sts. Join with a slip st to first sc. Change to D. Ch 1.

Continued on next page.

HAT

Make 6 motifs.

With RS facing, *and working through back loops only of last rnd,* whipstitch motifs tog into a ring.

Crown

Working along side edge of ring, with RS facing, attach B with a slip st to the first sc of any motif.

Rnd 1: Ch 3, work 15 dc along side of motif, *16 dc along side of next motif. Repeat from * around—96 sts. Join with a slip st to top of ch-3.

Rnd 2: Ch 3, dc into next 13 dc, *skip next 2 dc, dc into next 14 dc. Repeat from * around—84 sts. Join with a slip st to top of ch-3.

Rnd 3: Ch 3, dc into next 11 dc, *skip next 2 dc, dc into next 12 dc. Repeat from * around—72 sts. Join with a slip st to top of ch-3.

Rnd 4: Ch 3, dc into next 9 dc, *skip next 2 dc, dc into next 10 dc. Repeat from * around—60 sts. Join with a slip st to top of ch-3.

SKILL LEVEL
Intermediate

SIZES
One size fits all

MATERIALS
Classic Elite's *Provence* (sport weight; 100% cotton; each approx 4½ oz/125 g and 256 yd/233 m), 1 hank *each* of Mulberry #2632 (A), Purple #2656 (B), Grape #2652 (C), and Fuchsia #2634 (D)

Crochet hook, size F/5 (3.75 mm) or size needed to obtain gauge

Rnd 7: Sc into same st as slip st, sc into next 4 sc, *3 sc into next sc, sc into next 10 sc. Repeat from * around, ending rnd with 3 sc into next sc, sc into next 5 sc—52 sts. Join with a slip st to first sc. Ch 1.

Rnd 8: Sc into same st as slip st, sc into next 5 sc, *3 sc into next sc, sc into next 12 sc. Repeat from * around, ending rnd with 3 sc into next sc, sc into next 6 sc—60 sts. Join with a slip st to first sc.

Fasten off.

NOTES

Throughout, each sc, dc, and ch-3 counts as 1 st.

Since this hat is worked in the round, RS always faces you.

Rnd 5: Ch 3, dc into next 7 dc, *skip next 2 dc, dc into next 8 dc. Repeat from * around—48 sts. Join with a slip st to top of ch-3.

Rnd 6: Ch 3, dc into next 5 dc, *skip next 2 dc, dc into next 6 dc. Repeat from * around—36 sts. Join with a slip st to top of ch-3.

Rnd 7: Ch 3, dc into next 3 dc, *skip next 2 dc, dc into next 4 dc. Repeat from * around—24 sts. Join with a slip st to top of ch-3.

Rnd 8: Ch 3, dc into next dc, *skip next 2 dc, dc into next 2 dc. Repeat from * around—12 sts. Join with a slip st to top of ch-3.

Fasten off, leaving a long tail.

Weave yarn tail through last rnd and gather tightly to close top of hat.

Lower Edging

Working along lower edge of hat, with RS facing, attach B with a slip st to the first sc of any motif, and ch 1.

Rnd 1: Work 16 sc along side of motif, *16 sc along side of next motif. Repeat from * around—96 sts. Join with a slip st to first sc. Ch 1.

Rnd 2: Sc into same sc as slip st, ch 3, 4 dc into same sc as slip st, skip next 3 sc, sc into next sc, * ch 3, 4 dc into same sc as last sc, skip next 3 sc, sc into next sc. Repeat from * around, ending rnd with ch 3, 4 dc into same sc as last sc, skip next 3 sc, join with a slip st to first sc.

Fasten off.

COOL TIP This motif pattern offers endless color possibilities! Try crocheting motifs alternating two coordinating colors instead of four, or make each motif in a different solid color.

Fiona

This elegant dress doesn't miss a curve. Shaped to fit, it's trimmed with pretty touches of peek-a-boo lace.

GAUGE

In Solid Dc Patt with larger hook, 20 sts and 10 rows = 4". To measure your gauge, make a test swatch as follows: Ch 22. Work Solid Dc Patt on 20 sts for 10 rows total. Fasten off. Piece should measure 4" square. **To save time, take time to check gauge.**

SOLID DOUBLE CROCHET PATTERN

(any number of sts)

Foundation Row (RS): Dc into fourth ch from hook and into each ch across. Ch 3, turn.

Patt Row: Skip first dc, *dc into next dc. Repeat from * across, ending row with dc into top of turning-ch-3. Ch 3, turn.

Repeat Patt Row for patt.

NOTES

Throughout, each dc, dec dc, and turning-ch-3 counts as 1 st.

To decrease 1 st each side: Ch 3 to turn, skip first dc, work a dec dc to combine the next 2 dc, cont across until 3 sts rem in row, ending row with dec dc to combine the next 2 dc, dc into top of turning-ch-3. Ch 3, turn.

To increase 1 st each side: 2 dc into first dc, dc into each dc across, ending row with 2 dc into top of turning-ch-3. Ch 3, turn.

Continued on next page.

BACK

With larger hook, ch 115 (115, 129, 129).

Beg Solid Dc Patt, and work even on 113 (113, 127, 127) sts for 2 rows. Ch 3, turn.

Next Row (RS): Skip first dc, dc into next 3 dc, ch 4, split dec tr, ch 4, *dc into next 7 dc, ch 4, split dec tr, ch 4. Repeat from * across, ending row with dc into next 3 dc, dc into top of turning-ch-3. Ch 3, turn.

Next Row: Skip first dc, dc into next 3 dc, ch 7, *dc into next 7 dc, ch 7. Repeat from * across, ending row with dc into next 3 dc, dc into top of turning-ch-3. Ch 3, turn.

Next Row: Skip first dc, dc into next 3 dc, ch 4, sc under center of split dec tr two rows below, ch 4, *dc into next 7 dc, ch 4, sc under center of split dec tr two rows below, ch 4. Repeat from * across, ending row with dc into next 3 dc, dc into top of turning-ch-3. Ch 3, turn.

Next Row: Skip first dc, dc into next 3 dc, tr into next sc, ch 5, tr into same sc as last tr, *dc into next 7 dc, tr into next sc, ch 5, tr into same sc as last tr. Repeat from * across, ending row with dc into next 3 dc, dc into top of turning-ch-3. Ch 3, turn.

SKILL LEVEL
Intermediate

SIZES
Small (Medium, Large, Extra-Large). *Instructions are for smallest size, with changes for other sizes noted in parentheses as necessary.*

FINISHED MEASUREMENTS
Bust: 30 (33¼, 36½, 40½)"
Total length (excluding straps): 41"

MATERIALS
Plymouth's *Wildflower* (light worsted weight; 51% cotton/ 49% acrylic; each approx 1¾ oz/50 g and 136 yd/ 124 m), 16 (18, 20, 22) balls Royal Purple #14

Crochet hooks, sizes D/3 and E/4 (3.25 and 3.50 mm) or size needed to obtain gauge

Decrease double crochet = dec dc = Yarn over hook, insert hook into next st and pull up a loop (3 loops are on your hook); yarn over hook and draw loop through 2 loops on hook (2 loops are on your hook); yarn over hook, insert hook into next st and pull up a loop (4 loops are on your hook); yarn over hook and draw loop through 2 loops on hook; yarn over hook and draw loop through all 3 loops on hook.

Split decrease triple crochet = split dec tr = (Yarn over hook) twice, insert hook into next st and pull up a loop, (yarn over hook and draw loop through 2 loops) twice; skip next 5 sts, (yarn over hook) twice, insert hook into next st and pull up a loop, (yarn over hook and draw loop through 2 loops) twice; yarn over hook and draw loop through all 3 loops on hook.

Decrease single crochet = dec sc = (Insert hook into next st and pull up a loop) twice, yarn over hook and draw loop through all 3 loops on hook.

Next Row: Skip first dc, dc into next 3 dc, dc into next tr, 5 dc into ch-5 sp, dc into next tr, *dc into next 7 dc, dc into next tr, 5 dc into ch-5 sp, dc into next tr. Repeat from * across, ending row with dc into next 3 dc, dc into top of turning-ch-3— 113 (113, 127, 127) sts total. Ch 3, turn.

Cont even in patt until piece measures approx 15" from beg, ending after WS row. Ch 3, turn.

Shape Body
Dec 1 st each side every fourth row 0 (2, 0, 3) times, every other row 20 (18, 21, 16) times, then every row 4 (0, 2, 0) times—65 (73, 81, 89) sts rem. Ch 3, turn.

Cont even in patt until piece measures approx 35" from beg, ending after WS row. Ch 3, turn.

Inc 1 st each side every other row 3 (3, 3, 5) times, then every fourth row 1 (1, 1, 0) times—73 (81, 89, 99) sts.

Next Row (RS): Skip first dc, dc into next 4 (8, 5, 3) dc, ch 4, split dec tr, ch 4, *dc into next 7 dc, ch 4, split dec tr, ch 4. Repeat from * across, ending row with dc into next 4 (8, 5, 3) dc, dc into top of turning-ch-3. Ch 3, turn.

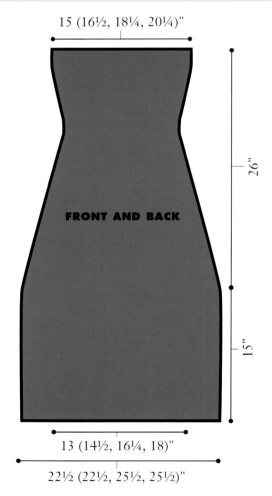

15 (16½, 18¼, 20¼)"

26"

FRONT AND BACK

15"

13 (14½, 16¼, 18)"

22½ (22½, 25½, 25½)"

Note: Measurements in schematic drawing do not include edging or shoulder straps.

Next Row: Skip first dc, dc into next 4 (8, 5, 3) dc, ch 7, *dc into next 7 dc, ch 7. Repeat from * across, ending row with dc into next 4 (8, 5, 3) dc, dc into top of turning-ch-3. Ch 3, turn.

Next Row: Skip first dc, dc into next 4 (8, 5, 3) dc, ch 4, sc under center of split dec tr two rows below, ch 4, *dc into next 7 dc, ch 4, sc under center of split dec tr two rows below, ch 4. Repeat from * across, ending row with dc into next 4 (8, 5, 3) dc, dc into top of turning-ch-3. Ch 3, turn.

Next Row: Dc into first dc, dc into next 4 (8, 5, 3) dc, tr into next sc, ch 5, tr into same sc as last tr, *dc into next 7 dc, tr into next sc, ch 5, tr into same sc as last tr. Repeat from * across, ending row with dc into next 4 (8, 5, 3) dc, 2 dc into top of turning-ch-3. Ch 3, turn.

Next Row: Skip first dc, dc into next 5 (9, 6, 4) dc, dc into next tr, 5 dc into ch-5 sp, dc into next tr, *dc into next 7 dc, dc into next tr, 5 dc into ch-5 sp, dc into next tr. Repeat from * across, ending row with dc into next 5 (9, 6, 4) dc, dc into top of turning-ch-3— 75 (83, 91, 101) sts.

Fasten off.

FRONT
Same as back.

FINISHING
Sew side seams, leaving 12" unsewn at lower left edge for side slit.

Lower Edging
With RS facing and smaller hook, attach yarn with a slip st to lower edge of back and ch 1.

Work 113 (113, 127, 127) sc along lower edge of back, 113 (113, 127, 127) sc along lower edge of front, 3 sc into lower left front corner, 59 sc along front edge of slit, dec sc at top of slit, and 59 sc along back edge of slit—348 (348, 362, 362) sts total. Join with a slip st to first sc.

Fasten off.

Upper Edging
With RS facing and smaller hook, attach yarn with a slip st to neck edge of left side seam and ch 1.

Rnd 1 (RS): Work 150 (165, 180, 201) sc evenly spaced around upper edge. Join with a slip st to first sc. *Do not turn.*

Rnd 2: *Working into front loops only,* *ch 3, dc into same sc as last slip st, skip next 2 sc, slip st into next sc. Repeat from * around, ending rnd with ch 3, dc into same sc as last slip st, skip next 2 sc, join with a slip st to first slip st.

Fasten off.

Shoulder straps *(Make 2)*
With smaller hook, ch 80.

Row 1 (WS): Dc into fourth ch from hook and into each ch across—38 sts. Ch 1, turn.

Row 2: Sc into each dc across; *working along side of Row 1,* work 3 slip sts; ch 1, then *working into unused loops of foundation chain,* sc into each dc across; *working along other side of Row 1,* work 3 slip sts—162 sts total. Join with a slip st to first sc.

Fasten off.

Sew shoulder straps to front and back approx 2½" in from each side seam, whipstitching them onto unused loops of Row 2 of Upper Edging and crossing them in the back.

COOL TIP If you prefer uncrossed straps, chain just long enough for the straps to fit comfortably over the shoulder. Attach them at the same spot on the front and back of the dress.

Rebecca

This citrus-colored scarf will brighten up any outfit. The mesh pattern is quick and easy to do, but that can be your little secret!

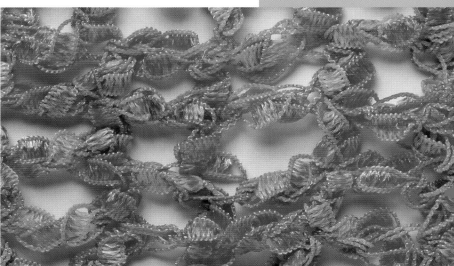

GAUGE

In Mesh Patt, 26 sts and 12 rows = 4". To measure your gauge, make a test swatch as follows: Ch 32. Work Mesh Patt on 28 sts for 12 rows total. Fasten off. Piece should measure 4½" wide and 4" high. **To save time, take time to check gauge.**

MESH PATTERN

(mult 3 + 1 sts)

Foundation Row (RS): Dc into eighth ch from hook, *ch 2, skip next 2 ch, dc into next ch. Repeat from * across. Ch 5, turn.

Patt Row: Skip first dc and ch-2 sp, *dc into next dc, ch 2, skip next ch-2 sp. Repeat from * across, ending row with skip next 2 ch, dc into next ch of turning-ch. Ch 5, turn.

Repeat Patt Row for patt.

NOTE

Throughout, each dc counts as 1 st; each ch-2 sp counts as 2 sts; each turning-ch-5 counts as 3 sts.

SCARF

Ch 32.

Beg Mesh Patt, and work even on 28 sts until piece measures approx 60" from beg.

Fasten off.

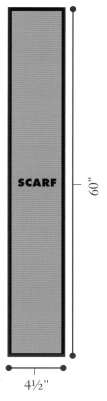

SCARF

60"

4½"

SKILL LEVEL
Advanced Beginner

SIZES
One size

FINISHED MEASUREMENTS
Approx 4½" wide and 60" long

MATERIALS
Trendsetter's *Binario* (light worsted weight; 100% polyamide; each approx . 90 oz/25 g and 82 yd/ 75 m), 2 balls Tropical Fruit #125

Crochet hook, size G/6 (4.00 mm) or size needed to obtain gauge

COOL TIP To keep the side edges of this scarf perfectly straight, be sure to work the last stitch of every row into the correct chain of the turning-chain.

Stacy

Dressed up or dressed down, you'll love this elegant pullover.

GAUGE

In Singles and Doubles Patt, 16 sts and 12 rows = 4". To measure your gauge, make a test swatch as follows: Ch 17. Work Singles and Doubles Patt on 16 sts for 12 rows total. Fasten off. Piece should measure 4" square. **To save time, take time to check gauge.**

SINGLES AND DOUBLES PATTERN

(any number of sts)

Foundation Row (WS): Sc into second ch from hook and into each ch across. Ch 3, turn.

Row 1 (RS): Skip first sc, dc into each sc across. Ch 1, turn.

Row 2: Sc into first dc and into each dc across, ending row with sc into top of turning-ch-3. Ch 3, turn.

Repeat Rows 1 and 2 for patt.

NOTES

Throughout, each sc, dc, dec sc, dec dc, and turning-ch-3 counts as 1 st.

To decrease 1 st each side on sc rows, ch 1 to turn; sc into first dc, work a dec sc to combine next 2 sts; cont across row until 3 sts rem, ending row with dec sc to combine next 2 sts, sc into top of turning-ch-3. Ch 3, turn.

To decrease 1 st each side on dc rows, ch 3 to turn; skip first st, work a dec dc to combine next 2 sts; cont across row until 3 sts rem, ending row with dec dc to combine next 2 sts, dc into last sc. Ch 1, turn.

Continued on next page.

BACK

Ch 71 (79, 89, 97, 105, 115).

Beg Singles and Doubles Patt, and work even on 70 (78, 88, 96, 104, 114) sts until piece measures approx 1" from beg.

Shape Body

Cont patt as established, and dec 1 st each side every other row 6 times—58 (66, 76, 84, 92, 102) sts.

Cont even in patt as established until piece measures approx 8" from beg.

Cont patt as established, and inc 1 st each side every other row 6 times—70 (78, 88, 96, 104, 114) sts.

Cont even, if necessary, in patt as established until piece measures approx 12½" from beg.

Shape Raglan

Cont patt as established, and dec 1 st each side every row 10 (6, 3, 4, 2, 1) times, then dec 2 sts each side every row 4 (8, 12, 13, 16, 19) times—34 (34, 34, 36, 36, 36) sts. Fasten off.

FRONT

Same as back until 46 (46, 46, 48, 48, 48) sts rem.

Use safety pins to mark the center 30 (30, 30, 32, 32, 32) sts.

SKILL LEVEL
Advanced Beginner

SIZES
Small (Medium, Large, Extra-Large, Extra-Extra-Large, Extra-Extra-Extra-Large). *Instructions are for smallest size, with changes for other sizes noted in parentheses as necessary.*

FINISHED MEASUREMENTS
Bust: 35 (39, 44, 48, 52, 57)"
Total length: 20 (20, 20½, 21, 21½, 22)"

MATERIALS
Classic Elite's *Flash* (heavy worsted weight; 100% mercerized cotton; each approx 1¾ oz/50 g and 93 yd/85 m), 10 (11, 11, 12, 12, 13) hanks Lotus Blossom #6127

Crochet hook, size G/6 (4.00 mm) or size needed to obtain gauge

Two safety pins

To decrease 2 sts each side on sc rows, ch 1 to turn; sc into first dc, (work a dec sc to combine next 2 sts) twice; cont across row until 5 sts rem, ending row with (dec sc to combine next 2 sts) twice, sc into top of turning-ch-3. Ch 3, turn.

To decrease 2 sts each side on dc rows, ch 3 to turn; skip first st, (work a dec dc to combine next 2 sts) twice; cont across row until 5 sts rem, ending row with (dec dc to combine next 2 sts) twice, dc into last sc. Ch 1, turn.

To increase 1 st each side on sc rows, ch 1, turn; sc into first dc, 2 sc into next dc; cont across row until 2 sts rem, ending row with 2 sc into next dc, sc into top of turning-ch-3. Ch 3, turn.

To increase 1 st each side on dc rows, ch 3, turn; skip first sc, 2 dc into next sc; cont across row until 2 sts rem, ending row with 2 dc into next sc, dc into last sc. Ch 1, turn.

Decrease single crochet = dec sc= (Insert hook into next st and pull up a loop) twice, yarn over hook and draw loop through all 3 loops on hook.

Decrease double crochet = dec dc = Yarn over hook, insert hook into next st and pull up a loop (3 loops are on your hook); yarn over hook and draw loop through 2 loops on hook (2 loops are on your hook); yarn over hook, insert hook into next st and pull up a loop (4 loops are on your hook); yarn over hook and draw loop through 2 loops on hook; yarn over hook and draw loop through all 3 loops on hook.

For sweater assembly, refer to the illustration for raglan construction on page 126.

Shape Neck

Next Row: Cont raglan shaping same as back, and work patt as established to first marked st. Chain to turn, leaving rest of row unworked.

Cont raglan shaping same as back, ***and at the same time,*** dec 1 st at neck edge every row twice.

For second side of neck, with RS facing, skip the middle 30 (30, 30, 32, 32, 32) sts, and attach yarn with a slip st to next st. Complete same as first side.

SLEEVES

Ch 53 (53, 55, 57, 61, 61).

Beg Singles and Doubles Patt on 52 (52, 54, 56, 60, 60) sts, and dec 1 st each side every other row 0 (0, 0, 1, 0, 2) times, then dec 1 st each side every row 14 (14, 15, 15, 18, 16) times—24 sts. Fasten off.

FINISHING

Sew raglan seams. Sew sleeve and side seams.

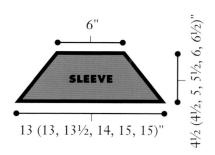

COOL TIP To prevent the holes next to turning-chains that often result when working into the second stitch of double crochet rows, work "linked double crochet stitches" as follows: Immediately following the turning-chain, insert the hook into the second chain of the turning-chain just made, then yarn over hook and draw the loop through the chain—two loops will be on your hook. Then, insert the hook into the next stitch the regular way (that is, into the second stitch of the row), yarn over hook and pull up a loop—three loops will be on your hook. Finally, complete the double crochet stitch as follows: (yarn over hook and draw loop through two loops on your hook) *twice.*

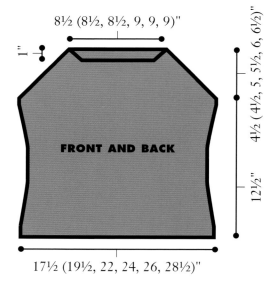

8½ (8½, 8½, 9, 9, 9)"

1"

4½ (4½, 5, 5½, 6, 6½)"

FRONT AND BACK

12½"

17½ (19½, 22, 24, 26, 28½)"

6"

SLEEVE

13 (13, 13½, 14, 15, 15)"

4½ (4½, 5, 5½, 6, 6½)"

Suzanne

This isn't your typical sweatshirt! This zippered hoodie is worked in an openwork cable stitch pattern in a beautiful cotton tape. It's casual yet sophisticated.

GAUGE

In Crossed St Patt, 16 sts and 10 rows = 4". To measure your gauge, make a test swatch as follows: Ch 18. Work Crossed St Patt on 17 sts for 10 rows total. Fasten off. Piece should measure 4¼" wide and 4" high. **To save time, take time to check gauge.**

CROSSED STITCH PATTERN

(mult 3 + 2 sts)

Foundation Row (WS): Sc into second ch from hook and into each ch across. Ch 3, turn.

Row 1 (RS): Skip first 3 sc, tr into next sc, ch 1, *working in front of last tr*, tr into second skipped sc, *skip next 2 sc, tr into next sc, ch 1, *working in front of last tr*, tr into first skipped sc. Repeat from * across, ending row with dc into last sc. Ch 1, turn.

Row 2: Sc into first dc, *sc into next tr, sc into ch-1 sp, sc into next tr. Repeat from * across, ending row with sc into top of turning-ch-3. Ch 3, turn.

Repeat Rows 1 and 2 for patt.

REVERSE SINGLE CROCHET PATTERN

(any number of sts)

Patt Row (RS): Working from left to right, sc into each st.

Continued on next page.

BACK

Ch 69 (75, 81, 93, 99).

Beg Crossed St Patt, and work even on 68 (74, 80, 92, 98) sts until piece measures approx 12½ (12½, 14, 13½, 13)" from beg, ending after Row 2 of patt. *Do not ch 3.* Turn.

Shape Armholes

Decrease Row 1 (RS): Slip st into first 4 (7, 7, 10, 10) sts, ch 3, skip st where last slip st was worked, cont patt as established across next 60 (60, 66, 72, 78) sts, ending row with dc into next st. Ch 1, turn, leaving rest of row unworked.

Decrease Row 2: Dec sc to combine dc and first tr, sc into each st across until 2 sts rem in row, ending row with dec sc to combine next tr and top of turning-ch-3. Ch 3, turn.

Decrease Row 3: Skip first st, dec dc to combine next 2 sts, *skip next 2 sc, tr into next sc, ch 1, *working in front of last tr*, tr into first skipped sc. Repeat from * across, ending row with dc into next sc, dec dc to combine the last 2 sts. Ch 1, turn.

SKILL LEVEL
Advanced

SIZES
Small (Medium, Large, Extra-Large, Extra-Extra-Large). *Instructions are for smallest size, with changes for other sizes noted in parentheses as necessary.*

FINISHED MEASUREMENTS
Bust (zipped): 34 (37, 40, 46, 49)"
Total length: 20 (20, 22, 22, 22)"

MATERIALS
Aurora Yarn/Ornaghi Filati's *Giglio* (heavy worsted weight; 100% mercerized cotton tape; each approx 1¾ oz/50 g and 88 yd/ 80 m), 17 (18, 20, 21, 22) balls Orchid #306

Crochet hook, size H/8 (5.00 mm) or size needed to obtain gauge

One 18 (18, 20, 20, 20)" separating zipper

NOTES

Throughout, each sc, dc, tr, ch-1 sp, and turning-ch-3 counts as 1 st.

Decrease single crochet = dec sc = (Insert hook into next st and pull up a loop) twice, yarn over hook and draw loop through all 3 loops on hook.

Decrease double crochet = dec dc = Yarn over hook, insert hook into next st and pull up a loop (3 loops are on your hook); yarn over hook and draw loop through 2 loops on hook (2 loops are on your hook); yarn over hook, insert hook into next st and pull up a loop (4 loops are on your hook); yarn over hook and draw loop through 2 loops on hook; yarn over hook and draw loop through all 3 loops on hook.

For sweater assembly, refer to the illustration for set-in construction on page 126.

Decrease Row 4: Dec sc to combine dec dc and next dc, *sc into next tr, sc into ch-1 sp, sc into next tr. Repeat from * across, ending row with dec sc to combine next dec dc and top of turning-ch-3. Ch 3, turn.

Decrease Row 5: Skip first st, *skip next 2 sc, tr into next sc, ch 1, *working in front of last tr*, tr into first skipped sc. Repeat from * across, ending row with dc into last st. Ch 1, turn—56 (56, 62, 68, 74) sts rem.

Repeat Armhole Decrease Rows 2-5 1 (1, 2, 2, 3) more times—50 (50, 50, 56, 56) sts rem.

Cont even in patt as established until piece measures approx 20 (20, 22, 22, 22)" from beg.

Fasten off.

LEFT FRONT

Ch 36 (39, 42, 48, 51).

Beg Crossed St Patt, and work even on 35 (38, 41, 47, 50) sts until piece measures approx 12½ (12½, 14, 13½, 13)" from beg, ending after Row 2 of patt. *Do not ch 3.* Turn.

Shape Armhole
Decrease Row 1 (RS): Slip st into first 4 (7, 7, 10, 10) sts, ch 3, skip st where last slip st was worked, cont patt as established across to end row. Ch 1, turn.

Decrease Row 2: Sc into each st across until 2 sts rem, ending row with dec sc to combine next tr and top of turning-ch-3. Ch 3, turn.

Decrease Row 3: Skip first st, dec dc to combine next 2 sts, *skip next 2 sc, tr into next sc, ch 1, *working in front of last tr*, tr into first skipped sc. Repeat from * across, ending row with dc into last sc. Ch 1, turn.

Decrease Row 4: Sc into each st across until 2 sts rem, ending row with dec sc to combine next dec dc and top of turning-ch-3. Ch 3, turn.

Decrease Row 5: Skip first st, *skip next 2 sc, tr into next sc, ch 1, *working in front of last tr*, tr into first skipped sc. Repeat from * across, ending row with dc into last st—29 (29, 32, 35, 38) sts rem. Ch 1, turn.

Repeat Armhole Decrease Rows 2-5 1 (1, 2, 2, 3) more times—26 (26, 26, 29, 29) sts rem.

Cont even in patt as established until piece measures approx 18 (18, 20, 20, 20)" from beg, ending after Row 2 of patt. Ch 3, turn.

Shape Neck
Decrease Row 1 (RS): Skip first sc, *skip next 2 sc, tr into next sc, ch 1, *working in front of last tr*, tr into first skipped sc. Repeat from * across until 13 sts rem in row, ending row with dc into next st. Ch 1, turn, leaving rest of row unworked.

Decrease Row 2: Dec sc to combine first dc and tr, sc into each st across, ending row with sc into top of turning-ch-3. Ch 3, turn.

Decrease Row 3: Skip first sc, *skip next 2 sc, tr into next sc, ch 1, *working in front of last tr*, tr into first skipped sc. Repeat from * across, ending row with dc into next sc, dec dc to combine the last 2 sts. Ch 1, turn.

Decrease Row 4: Dec sc to combine first 2 sts, sc into each st across, ending row with sc into top of turning-ch-3—11 (11, 11, 14, 14) sts rem. Ch 3, turn.

Cont even, if necessary, in patt as established until piece measures same as back to shoulders.

Fasten off.

RIGHT FRONT

Same as left front until piece measures same as left front to armhole, ending after Row 2 of patt. Ch 3, turn.

Shape Armhole
Decrease Row 1 (RS): Skip first sc, *skip next 2 sc, tr into next sc, ch 1, *working in front of last tr*, tr into first skipped sc. Repeat from * across until 4 (7, 7, 10, 10) sts rem in row, ending row with dc into next st. Ch 1, turn, leaving rest of row unworked.

Decrease Row 2: Dec sc to combine first 2 sts, sc into each st across, ending row with sc into top of turning-ch-3. Ch 3, turn.

Decrease Row 3: Skip first st, *skip next 2 sc, tr into next sc, ch 1, *working in front of last tr*; tr into first skipped sc. Repeat from * across, ending row with dc into next sc, dec dc to combine last 2 sts. Ch 1, turn.

Decrease Row 4: Dec sc to combine first 2 sts, sc into each st across, ending row with sc into top of turning-ch-3. Ch 3, turn.

Decrease Row 5: Skip first st, *skip next 2 sc, tr into next sc, ch 1, *working in front of last tr*; tr into first skipped sc. Repeat from * across, ending row with dc into last st—29 (29, 32, 35, 38) sts rem. Ch 1, turn.

Repeat Armhole Decrease Rows 2-5 1 (1, 2, 2, 3) more times—26 (26, 26, 29, 29) sts rem.

Cont even in patt as established until piece measures approx 18 (18, 20, 20, 20)" from beg, ending after Row 2 of patt. *Do not ch 3.* Turn.

Shape Neck
Decrease Row 1 (RS): Slip st into first 13 sts, ch 3, skip st where last slip st was worked, cont patt as established across to end row. Ch 1, turn.

Decrease Row 2: Sc into each st across until 2 sts rem in row, ending row with dec sc to combine last 2 sts. Ch 3, turn.

Decrease Row 3: Skip first sc, dec dc to combine next 2 sts, *skip next 2 sc, tr into next sc, ch 1, *working in front of last tr*; tr into first skipped sc. Repeat from * across, ending row with dc into last sc. Ch 1, turn.

Decrease Row 4: Sc into first dc, *sc into next tr, sc into ch-1 sp, sc into next tr. Repeat from * across, ending row with dec sc to combine next dec dc and top of turning-ch-3—11 (11, 11, 14, 14) sts rem. Ch 3, turn.

Complete same as left front.

SLEEVES
Ch 36 (36, 39, 42, 45).

Beg Crossed St Patt, and work even on 35 (35, 38, 41, 44) sts for 2 rows. Ch 1, turn.

Next Row (WS): 2 sc into first dc, *sc into next tr, sc into ch-1 sp, sc into next tr. Repeat from * across, ending row with 2 sc into top of turning-ch-3. Ch 3, turn.

Next Row: Skip first sc, dc into next sc, *skip next 2 sc, tr into next sc, ch 1, *working in front of last tr*; tr into first skipped sc. Repeat from * across, ending row with dc into last 2 sc. Ch 1, turn.

Next Row: 2 sc into first dc, sc into next dc, *sc into next tr, sc into ch-1 sp, sc into next tr. Repeat from * across, ending row with sc into next dc, 2 sc into top of turning-ch-3. Ch 3, turn.

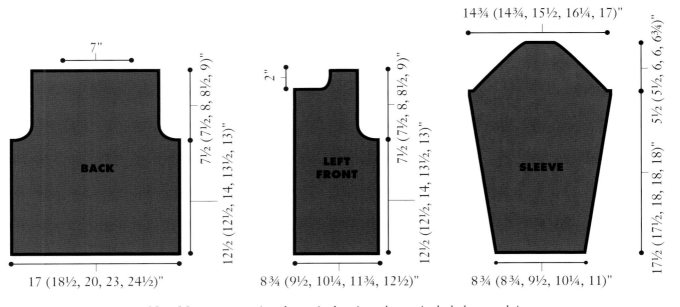

Note: Measurements in schematic drawings do not include lower edging.

Next Row: Skip first 2 sc, tr into next sc, ch 1, *working in front of last tr*, tr into last skipped sc, *skip next 2 sc, tr into next sc, ch 1, *working in front of last tr*, tr into first skipped sc. Repeat from * across, ending row with skip next sc, tr into next sc, ch 1, *working in front of last tr*, tr into skipped sc, dc into last sc. Ch 1, turn.

Cont even on 41 (41, 44, 47, 50) sts in patt as established for 6 rows. Ch 1, turn.

Repeat last 10 rows 3 more times—59 (59, 62, 65, 68) sts. Ch 1, turn.

Cont even in patt as established until piece measures approx 17½ (17½, 18, 18, 18)" from beg, ending after Row 2 of patt. *Do not ch 3.* Turn.

Shape Cap
Next Row (RS): Slip st into first 4 (7, 7, 10, 10) sts, ch 3, skip st where last slip st was worked, cont patt as established across next 51 (45, 48, 45, 48) sts, ending row with dc into next st—53 (47, 50, 47, 50) sts. Ch 1, turn, leaving rest of row unworked.

Cont even in patt as established for 0 (0, 2, 2, 4) rows—53 (47, 50, 47, 50) sts. Ch 1, turn.

Next Row: Dec sc to combine first dc and tr, dec sc to combine ch-1 sp and next tr, *sc into next tr, sc into next ch-1 sp, sc into next tr. Repeat from * across until 4 sts rem in row, ending row with dec sc to combine next tr and ch-1 sp, dec sc to combine next tr and top of turning-ch-3. Ch 3, turn.

Next Row: Skip first sc, dc into next st, dec dc to combine next 2 sc, dc into next sc, *skip next 2 sc, tr into next sc, ch 1, *working in front of last tr*, tr into first skipped sc. Repeat from * across until 5 sts rem in row, ending row with dc into next sc, (dec dc to combine next 2 sts) twice. Ch 1, turn.

Next Row: Dec sc to combine first 2 dec sts, dec sc to combine next dc and tr, sc into next ch-1 sp, sc into next tr, *sc into next tr, sc into next ch-1 sp, sc into next tr. Repeat from * across until 7 sts rem in row, ending row with sc into next tr, sc into next ch-1 sp, dec sc to combine next tr and dc, dec sc to combine next dec dc and turning-ch-3, skipping 1 dc. Ch 3, turn.

Next Row: Skip first st, dc into next st, dec dc to combine next 2 sc, *skip next 2 sc, tr into next sc, ch 1, *working in front of last tr*, tr into first skipped sc. Repeat from * across until 4 sts rem in row, ending row with (dec dc to combine next 2 sts) twice. Ch 1, turn.

Next Row: Dec sc to combine first 2 sts, dec sc to combine next tr and ch-1 sp, sc into next tr, *sc into next tr, sc into next ch-1 sp, sc into next tr. Repeat from * across until 6 sts rem in row, ending row with sc into next tr, dec sc to combine ch-1 sp and next tr, dec sc to combine next dec dc and top of turning-ch-3, skipping 1 dc. Ch 3, turn.

Next Row: Skip first st, dc into next st, dec dc to combine next 2 sc, dc into next 2 sc, *skip next 2 sc, tr into next sc, ch 1, *working in front of last tr*, tr into first skipped sc. Repeat from * across until 6 sts rem in row, ending row with dc into next 2 sc, (dec dc to combine next 2 sts) twice. Ch 1, turn.

Next Row: Dec sc to combine first 2 dec sts, dec sc to combine next 2 dc, *sc into next tr, sc into next ch-1 sp, sc into next tr. Repeat from * across until 5 sts rem in row, ending row with dec sc to combine next 2 dc, dec sc to combine next dec dc and top of turning-ch-3, skipping 1 dc. Ch 3, turn.

Next Row: Skip first sc, dc into next st, dec dc to combine next 2 sc, dc into next sc, *skip next 2 sc, tr into next sc, ch 1, *working in front of last tr*, tr into first skipped sc. Repeat from * across until 5 sts rem in row, ending row with dc into next sc, (dec dc to combine next 2 sts) twice. Ch 1, turn.

Next Row: Dec sc to combine first 2 dec sts, dec dc to combine next dc and tr, sc into next ch-1 sp, sc into next tr, *sc into next tr, sc into next ch-1 sp, sc into next tr. Repeat from * across until 7 sts rem in row, ending row with sc into next tr, sc into next ch-1 sp, dec sc to combine next tr and dc, dec sc to combine next dec dc and turning-ch-3, skipping 1 dc. Ch 3, turn.

Next Row: Skip first sc, dc into next st, dec dc to combine next 2 sc, *skip next 2 sc, tr into next sc, ch 1, *working in front of last tr*, tr into first skipped sc. Repeat from * across until 4 sts rem in row, ending row with (dec dc to combine next 2 sts) twice. Ch 1, turn.

Next Row: Dec sc to combine first 2 sts, dec sc to combine next tr and ch-1 sp, sc into next tr, *sc into next tr, sc into next ch-1 sp, sc into next tr. Repeat from * across, if necessary, until 6 sts rem in row, ending row with sc into next tr, dec sc to combine next ch-1 sp and tr, dec sc to combine next dec dc and turning-ch-3, skipping 1 dc—9 (3, 6, 3, 6) sts rem.

For Sizes Medium, Large, Extra-Large, and Extra-Extra-Large Only:
Next Row (RS): Cont even in patt as established.

Fasten off.

For Size Small Only:
Ch 3, turn.

Next Row: Skip first st, dec dc to combine next 2 sts, *skip next 2 sc, tr into next sc, ch 1, *working in front of last tr;* tr into first skipped sc. Repeat from * across until 3 sts rem in row, ending row with dc into next sc, dec dc to combine last 2 sts. Ch 1, turn.

Next Row: Dec sc to combine first 2 sts, *sc into next tr, sc into next ch-1 sp, sc into next tr. Repeat from * across until 3 sts rem in row, ending row with dec sc to combine next dec dc and top of turning-ch-3— 5 sts rem.

Fasten off.

FINISHING

Sew shoulder seams, joining 11 (11, 11, 14, 14) sts each side, leaving the middle 28 sts open for back of neck.

Hood

With RS facing, attach yarn with a slip st to beg of right front neck shaping and ch 1.

Work 68 sc evenly spaced around neck opening. Ch 1, turn.

Next Row (WS): Same as Foundation Row of Crossed St Patt—68 sts. Ch 3, turn.

Repeat Rows 1 and 2 of Crossed St Patt on 68 sts until hood measures approx 3" from beg, ending after Row 1 of patt. Ch 1, turn.

Next Row (WS): Sc into first dc, (sc into next tr, sc into ch-1 sp, sc into next tr) 9 times, sc into next tr, 2 sc into next ch-1 sp, sc into next 2 tr, (sc into next ch-1 sp, sc into next 2 tr) twice, 2 sc into next ch-1 sp, sc into next 2 tr, sc into next ch-1 sp, *sc into next 2 tr, sc into next ch-1 sp. Repeat from * across, ending row with sc into next tr, sc into top of turning-ch-3— 70 sts. Ch 3, turn.

Next Row: Skip first 3 sc, tr into next sc, ch 1, *working in front of last tr;* tr into second skipped sc, (skip next 2 sc, tr into next sc, ch 1, *working in front of last tr;* tr into first skipped sc) 8 times, skip next 2 sc, tr into next sc, ch 2, *working in front of last tr;* tr into first skipped sc, (skip next 2 sc, tr into next sc, ch 1, *working in front of last tr;* tr into first skipped sc) twice, skip next 2 sc, tr into next sc, ch 2, *working in front of last tr;* tr into first skipped sc, *skip next 2 sc, tr into next sc, ch 1, *working in front of last tr;* tr into first skipped sc. Repeat from * across, ending row with dc into last sc. Ch 1, turn.

Next Row: Sc into first dc, (sc into next tr, sc into ch-1 sp, sc into next tr) 9 times, sc into next tr, 4 sc into next ch-2 sp, sc into next 2 tr, sc into ch-1 sp, sc into next 2 tr, sc into ch-1 sp, sc into next 2 tr, 4 sc into next ch-2 sp, sc into next tr, *sc into next tr, sc into ch-1 sp, sc into next tr. Repeat from * across, ending row with sc into top of turning-ch-3—74 sts. Ch 3, turn.

Next Row: Skip first 3 sc, tr into next sc, ch 1, *working in front of last tr;* tr into second skipped sc, *skip next 2 sc, tr into next sc, ch 1, *working in front of last tr;* tr into first skipped sc. Repeat from * across, ending row with dc into last sc. Ch 1, turn.

Next Row: Sc into first dc, *sc into next tr, sc into ch-1 sp, sc into next tr. Repeat from * across, ending row with sc into top of turning-ch-3. Ch 3, turn.

Next Row: Skip first 3 sc, tr into next sc, ch 1, *working in front of last tr;* tr into second skipped sc, *skip next 2 sc, tr into next sc, ch 1, *working in front of last tr;* tr into first skipped sc. Repeat from * across, ending row with dc into last sc. Ch 1, turn.

Repeat last 2 rows until hood measures approx 11 (12, 12, 12, 12)" from beg, ending after RS row—74 sts. Ch 1, turn.

Next Row: Sc into first dc, (sc into next tr, sc into ch-1 sp, sc into next tr) 9 times, sc into next tr, (skip next ch-1 sp, sc into next 2 tr) twice, (sc into ch-1 sp, sc into next 2 tr) twice, (skip next ch-1 sp, sc into next 2 tr) twice, sc into next ch-1 sp, sc into next tr, *sc into next tr, sc into next ch-1 sp, sc into next tr. Repeat from * across, ending row with sc into top of turning-ch-3—70 sts rem. Ch 3, turn.

Next Row: Skip first sc, (skip next 2 sc, tr into next sc, ch 1, *working in front of last tr;* tr into first skipped sc) 9 times, skip next 3 sc, tr into next sc, ch 2, *working in front of last tr;* tr into first skipped sc, (skip next 2 sc, tr into next sc, ch 1, *working in front of last tr;* tr into first skipped sc) twice, skip next 3 sc, tr into

next sc, ch 2, *working in front of last tr;* tr into first skipped sc, *skip next 2 sc, tr into next sc, ch 1, *working in front of last tr;* tr into first skipped sc. Repeat from * across, ending row with dc into last sc—68 sts rem. Ch 1, turn.

Next Row: Sc into first dc, (sc into next tr, sc into ch-1 sp, sc into next tr) 9 times, sc into next tr, sc into next ch-2 sp, sc into next 2 tr, sc into ch-1 sp, sc into next 2 tr, sc into ch-1 sp, sc into next 2 tr, sc into next ch-2 sp, sc into next tr, *sc into next tr, sc into ch-1 sp, sc into next tr. Repeat from * across, ending row with sc into top of turning-ch-3—68 sts.

Fasten off.

Fold last row in half. With RS facing, sew tog to form top of hood.

Sleeve Edging
With RS facing, attach yarn with a slip st to lower edge of sleeve seam and ch 1.

Working into unused loops of foundation chain, work 1 row of sc evenly spaced along lower edge of sleeve. Ch 1. *Do not turn.*

Next Row (RS): Work 1 row of Reverse Sc Patt.

Fasten off.

Set in sleeves. Sew side and sleeve seams.

Lower Edging
With RS facing, attach yarn with a slip st to lower left front edge and ch 1.

Working into unused loops of foundation chain, work 1 row of sc evenly spaced along lower edge of left front, back, and right front. Ch 1. *Do not turn.*

Next Row (RS): Work 1 row of Reverse Sc Patt along lower edge of right front, back, and left front.

Fasten off.

Front Edging
With RS facing, attach yarn with a slip st to lower right front edge and ch 1.

Work 1 row of sc evenly spaced up right front edge, around hood, and down left front edge. Ch 1. *Do not turn.*

Next Row (RS): Work 1 row of Reverse Sc Patt up left front edge, around hood, and down right front edge.

Fasten off.

Sew in zipper.

Candace

Looking for a new fashion accessory? This perfectly sized clutch is fun to make, even for novices. Its nubby texture cleverly hides any uneven stitches.

GAUGE

In Solid Sc Patt, 7 sts and 7 rows = 4". To measure your gauge, make a test swatch as follows: Ch 8. Work Solid Sc Patt for 7 rows total. Fasten off. Piece should measure 4" square. **To save time, take time to check gauge.**

SOLID SINGLE CROCHET PATTERN

(any number of sts)

Foundation Row (RS): Sc into second ch from hook and into each ch across. Ch 1, turn.

Patt Row: Sc into each sc across. Ch 1, turn.

Repeat Patt Row for patt.

NOTES

Throughout, each sc and dec sc counts as 1 st.

Decrease single crochet = dec sc = (Insert hook into next st and pull up a loop) twice, yarn over hook and draw loop through all 3 loops on hook.

FRONT

Attach yarn with a slip st around one of the rods. Ch 1.

Row 1 (RS): Work 25 sc over rod. Ch 1, turn. *(See "Single Crochet Stitch Worked Over a Rod or Ring," below.)*

Row 2: Sc into each sc across—25 sts. Ch 1, turn.

Repeat last row until piece measures approx 6" from lower edge of rod.

Fasten off.

BACK

Same as front.

Gusset

Ch 4.

Row 1 (RS): Sc into second ch from hook and into each ch across—3 sts.

Ch 1, turn.

Rows 2 and 3: Sc into each sc across—3 sts. Ch 1, turn.

Row 4: Sc into first sc, 2 sc into next sc, sc into next sc—4 sts. Ch 1, turn.

SKILL LEVEL
Advanced Beginner

FINISHED MEASUREMENTS
Approx 12½" wide and 6" long

MATERIALS
Lion Brand's *Bouclé* (bulky weight; 79% acrylic/ 20% mohair/1% nylon; each approx 2½ oz/70 g and 57 yd/52 m), 3 balls Lime Blue #202

Crochet hook, size N/15 (10.00 mm) or size needed to obtain gauge

Two 12" Lucite rods (Judi & Co.'s *Style #LU-5* was used on sample project)

(Optional: coordinating fabric for lining)

SINGLE CROCHET STITCH WORKED OVER A ROD OR RING

Attach yarn with a slip stitch to a rod or ring, then work the required number of single crochet stitches *around* the rod or ring.

Rows 5 and 6: Sc into each sc across—4 sts. Ch 1, turn.

Row 7: Sc into first sc, 2 sc into next sc, sc into next 2 sc—5 sts. Ch 1, turn.

Rows 8-10: Sc into each sc across—5 sts. Ch 1, turn.

Place marker.

Repeat last row until piece measures approx 12½" from marker. Ch 1, turn.

Place second marker.

Next Three Rows: Sc into each sc across—5 sts. Ch 1, turn.

Next Row: Sc into first sc, dec sc to combine next 2 sts, sc into next 2 sc—4 sts rem. Ch 1, turn.

Next Two Rows: Sc into each sc across—4 sts. Ch 1, turn.

Next Row: Sc into first sc, dec sc to combine next 2 sts, sc into next st—3 sts rem. Ch 1, turn.

Next Two Rows: Sc into each sc across—3 sts. Ch 1, turn.

Next Row: Sc into each sc across—3 sts.

Fasten off.

COOL TIP For a different look, crochet your bag holding together one strand each of smooth worsted weight yarn and a coordinating novelty eyelash yarn. Simply adjust your hook size until you achieve the required gauge.

FINISHING

(*Optional:* Cut lining to fit bag. Fold ¼" hems to WS. Sew lining into place.)

With WS of front and back tog, and with RS of gusset facing you, pin lower edges of front and back to the side edges of gusset between markers.

Beg approx 1½" from lower edge of rods, pin the rest of gusset to side edges of front and back.

With RS facing, attach yarn with a slip st to upper edge of bag and work 1 row of sc evenly spaced through both layers of fabric to join edges of gusset and bag tog, working 3 sc into each bottom corner.

Fasten off.

Helene

Made from cotton yarn in bright, sassy colors, this little top is quick to make and easy to wear.

GAUGE

In Seed St Patt with larger hook, 28 sts and 24 rows = 4". To measure your gauge, make a test swatch as follows: With larger hook, ch 29. Work Seed St Patt on 28 sts for 24 rows total. Fasten off. Piece should measure 4" square. **To save time, take time to check gauge.**

SEED STITCH PATTERN
(mult 2 + 1 sts)

Foundation Row (RS): Sc into second ch from hook, *ch 1, skip next ch, sc into next ch. Repeat from * across. Ch 1, turn.

Row 1 (WS): Sc into first sc, *sc into next ch-1 sp, ch 1, skip next sc. Repeat from * across, ending row with sc into next ch-1 sp, sc into last sc. Ch 1, turn.

Row 2: Sc into first sc, *ch 1, skip next sc, sc into next ch-1 sp. Repeat from * across, ending row with ch 1, skip next sc, sc into last sc. Ch 1, turn.

Repeat Rows 1 and 2 for patt.

STRIPE PATTERN

*5 rows A, 1 row B, 5 rows C, 1 row B. Repeat from * for patt.

NOTES

Throughout, each sc, ch-1 sp, and dec sc counts as 1 st; each turning-ch-1 *does not* count as 1 st.

Decrease single crochet = dec sc = (Insert hook into next st and pull up a loop) twice, yarn over hook and draw loop through all 3 loops on hook.

BACK

With larger hook and A, ch 120 (134, 148, 162, 176).

Beg Seed St Patt, and work even on 119 (133, 147, 161, 175) sts in Stripe Patt until piece measures approx 11" from beg, ending after WS row. *Do not ch 1.* Turn.

Shape Armholes

Next Row (RS): Slip st into first 8 (14, 16, 22, 26) sts, ch 1, *sc into next ch-1 sp, ch 1, skip next sc. Repeat from * across until 8 (14, 16, 22, 26) sts rem in row—103 (105, 115, 117, 123) sts. Ch 1, turn, leaving rest of row unworked.

Next Row: Dec sc to combine first sc and ch-1 sp, *ch 1, skip next sc, sc into next ch-1 sp. Repeat from * across until 3 sts rem, ending row with ch 1, skip next sc, dec sc to combine next ch-1 sp and last sc—101 (103, 113, 115, 121) sts. Ch 1, turn.

Next Row: Dec sc to combine first dec sc and ch-1 sp, *ch 1, skip next sc, sc into next ch-1 sp. Repeat from * across until 3 sts rem, ending row with ch 1, skip next sc, dec sc to combine next ch-1 sp and next dec sc—99 (101, 111, 113, 119) sts. Ch 1, turn.

SKILL LEVEL
Intermediate

SIZES
Small (Medium, Large, Extra-Large, Extra-Extra-Large). *Instructions are for smallest size, with changes for other sizes noted in parentheses as necessary.*

FINISHED MEASUREMENTS
Bust: 34 (38, 42, 46, 50)"
Total length: 18 (18, 18½, 19, 19½)"

MATERIALS
Aurora Yarn/Ornaghi Filati's *Safran* (sport weight; 100% Egyptian cotton; each approx 1¾ oz/50 g and 175 yd/160 m, 3 (4, 4, 5, 5) balls Orange #28 (A), 2 (2, 3, 3, 4) balls Sunshine #11 (B), and 3 (3, 4, 4, 5) balls #13 Strawberry (C)

Crochet hook, sizes D/3 and E/4 (3.25 and 3.50 mm) or size needed to obtain gauge

Repeat last row 8 (8, 10, 10, 12) more times, maintaining Stripe Patt as established, dec 1 st each side of each row—83 (85, 91, 93, 95) sts. Ch 1, turn.

Cont even in patts as established until piece measures approx 17 (17, 17½, 18, 18½)" from beg, ending after WS row.

Shape Neck

Next Row (RS): Work Seed St Patt as established across first 19 (19, 21, 21, 21) sts, ch 1, turn.

Next Row: Dec sc to combine first sc and ch-1 sp, *ch 1, skip next sc, sc into next ch-1 sp. Repeat from * across, ending row with sc into last sc—18 (18, 20, 20, 20) sts. Ch 1, turn.

Next Row: Work Seed St Patt as established across first 16 (16, 18, 18, 18) sts, dec sc to combine next ch-1 sp and dec sc—17 (17, 19, 19, 19) sts. Ch 1, turn.

Cont even in patts as established until this side measures approx 18 (18, 18½, 19, 19½)" from beg.

Fasten off.

For second side of neck, with RS facing, maintaining Stripe Patt as established, skip the middle 45 (47, 49, 51, 53) sts and attach yarn with a slip st to next sc and ch 1, work Seed St Patt as established across 19 (19, 21, 21, 21) sts to end row. Ch 1, turn.

Next Row: Work patts as established across first 16 (16, 18, 18, 18) sts, ch 1, skip next sc, dec sc to combine next ch-1 sp and next sc—18 (18, 20, 20, 20) sts. Ch 1, turn.

Next Row: Dec sc to combine first dec sc and ch-1 sp, *ch 1, skip next sc, sc into next ch-1 sp. Repeat from * across, ending row with sc into last sc—17 (17, 19, 19, 19) sts. Ch 1, turn.

Complete same as first side.

Fasten off.

FRONT

Same as back until piece measures approx 13 (13, 13½, 14, 14½)" from beg, ending after WS row. Ch 1, turn.

Divide for Neck Slit and Shape Neck
For Sizes Small, Large, and Extra-Extra-Large Only:

Next Row (RS): Work Seed St Patt as established across first 39 (_, 43, _, 45) sts, sc into next sc. Ch 1, turn, leaving rest of row unworked—40 (_, 44, _, 46) sts.

Next Row: Sc into first sc, *ch 1, skip next sc, sc into next ch-1 sp. Repeat from * across, ending row with sc into last sc—40 (_, 44, _, 46) sts. Ch 1, turn.

Repeat last 2 rows, maintaining Stripe Patt as established, until piece measures approx 16 (_, 16½, _, 17½)" from beg, ending after WS row.

Next Row (RS): Work Seed St Patt as established across first 27 (_, 29, _, 29) sts, ch 1, turn.

Next Row: Dec sc to combine first sc and ch-1 sp, *ch 1, skip next sc, sc into next ch-1 sp. Repeat from * across, ending row with sc into last sc—26 (_, 28, _, 28) sts. Ch 1, turn.

Next Row: Work Seed St Patt as established until 2 sts rem this side, ending row with dec sc to combine next ch-1 sp and dec sc—25 (_, 27, _, 27) sts. Ch 1, turn.

Repeat last 2 rows, maintaining Stripe Patt as established, dec 1 st each side of each row, until 17 (_, 19, _, 19) sts rem. Ch 1, turn.

Cont even in patts as established until this side measures same as back to shoulders.

Fasten off.

For second side of neck, with RS facing, maintaining Stripe Patt as established, skip the middle 3 sts and attach yarn with a slip st to next sc and ch 1, sc into same sc as slip st, sc into next ch-1 sp, work Seed St Patt as established across to end row—40 (_, 44, _, 46) sts. Ch 1, turn.

Next Row: Sc into first sc, *sc into next ch-1 sp, ch 1, skip next sc. Repeat from * across, ending row with sc into last sc—40 (_, 44, _, 46) sts. Ch 1, turn.

Repeat last 2 rows, maintaining Stripe Patt as established, until piece measures approx 16 (_, 16½, _, 17½)" from beg, ending after WS row.

Fasten off.

With RS facing, maintaining Stripe Patt as established, skip the first 13 (_, 15, _, 17) sts on this side, and attach yarn with a slip st to next sc and ch 1, work in Seed St Patt as established to end row—27 (_, 29, _, 29) sts. Ch 1, turn.

Next Row: Work Seed St Pat as established until 3 sts rem, ending row with ch 1, skip next sc, dec sc to combine next ch-1 sp and last sc— 26 (_, 28, _, 28) sts. Ch 1, turn.

Next Row (RS): Dec sc to combine first sc and ch-1 sp, *ch 1, skip next sc, sc into next ch-1 sp. Repeat from * across, ending row with ch 1, skip next sc, sc into last sc—25 (_, 27, _, 27) sts. Ch 1, turn.

Repeat last 2 rows, maintaining Stripe Patt as established, dec 1 st each side of each row, until 17 (_, 19, _, 19) sts rem. Ch 1, turn.

Complete same as first side.

For Sizes Medium and Extra-Large Only:
Next Row (RS): Work Seed St Patt as established across first _ (41, _, 45, _) sts. Ch 1, turn, leaving rest of row unworked.

Next Row: Sc into first sc, sc into ch-1 sp, *ch 1, skip next sc, sc into next ch-1 sp. Repeat from * across, ending row with sc into last sc—_ (41, _, 45, _) sts. Ch 1, turn.

Repeat last 2 rows, maintaining Stripe Patt as established, until piece measures approx _ (16, _, 17, _)" from beg, ending after WS row.

Next Row (RS): Work Seed St Patt as established across first _ (27, _, 29, _) sts, ch 1, turn.

Next Row: Dec sc to combine first sc and ch-1 sp, *ch 1, skip next sc, sc into next ch-1 sp. Repeat from * across, ending row with sc into last sc—_ (26, _, 28, _) sts. Ch 1, turn.

Next Row: Work Seed St Patt as established until 2 sts rem this side, ending row with dec sc to combine next ch-1 sp and dec sc—_ (25, _, 27, _) sts. Ch 1, turn.

Repeat last 2 rows, maintaining Stripe Patt as established, dec 1 st each side of each row, until _ (17, _, 19, _) sts rem. Ch 1, turn.

Cont even in patts as established until this side measures same as back to shoulders.

Fasten off.

For second side of neck, with RS facing, maintaining Stripe Patt as established, skip the middle 3 sts and attach yarn with a slip st to next sc and ch 1, sc into same sc as slip st, work Seed St Patt as established across to end row—_ (41, _, 45, _) sts. Ch 1, turn.

Next Row: Sc into first sc, *sc into next ch-1 sp, ch 1, skip next sc. Repeat from * across, ending row with sc into last ch-1 sp, sc into last sc—_ (41, _, 45, _) sts. Ch 1, turn.

FINISHING

Sew shoulder and side seams.

Neckline Edging

With RS facing and smaller hook, attach A with a slip st to neck edge of right shoulder seam and ch 1. Work 1 rnd of sc evenly spaced around neckline, working 3 sc at beg of each front neck shaping and a dec sc at each lower edge of neck slit and at beg of each side of back neck shaping. Join with a slip st to first sc.

Fasten off.

Armhole Edging

With RS facing and smaller hook, attach A with a slip st to upper edge of right side seam and ch 1. Work 1 rnd of sc evenly spaced around armhole edge. Join with a slip st to first sc.

Fasten off.

Repeat for left armhole.

Lower Edging

With RS facing and smaller hook, attach A with a slip st to lower edge of right side seam and ch 1. Work 1 rnd of sc evenly spaced around bottom edge. Join with a slip st to first sc.

Fasten off.

Repeat last 2 rows, maintaining Stripe Patt as established, until piece measures approx _ (16, _, 17, _)" from beg, ending after WS row.

Fasten off.

With RS facing, maintaining Stripe Patt as established, skip the first _ (14, _, 16, _) sts on this side, and attach yarn with a slip st to next sc and ch 1.

Next Row (RS): Dec sc to combine first sc and ch-1 sp, sc into next ch-1 sp, *ch 1, skip next sc, sc into next ch-1 sp. Repeat from * across, ending row with ch 1, skip next sc, sc into last sc—_ (26, _, 28, _) sts. Ch 1, turn.

Next Row: Work Seed St Pat as established until 3 sts rem, ending row with ch 1, skip next sc, dec sc to combine next ch-1 sp and last sc— _ (25, _, 27, _) sts. Ch 1, turn.

Repeat last 2 rows, maintaining Stripe Patt as established, dec 1 st each side of each row, until _ (17, _, 19, _) sts rem. Ch 1, turn.

Complete same as first side.

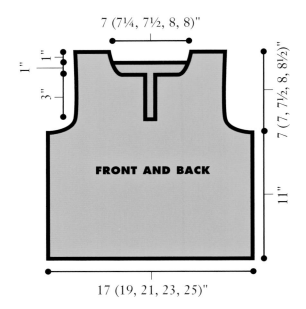

7 (7¼, 7½, 8, 8)"

1"

1"

3"

7 (7, 7½, 8, 8½)"

FRONT AND BACK

11"

17 (19, 21, 23, 25)"

Note: Measurements in schematic drawing do not include edging.

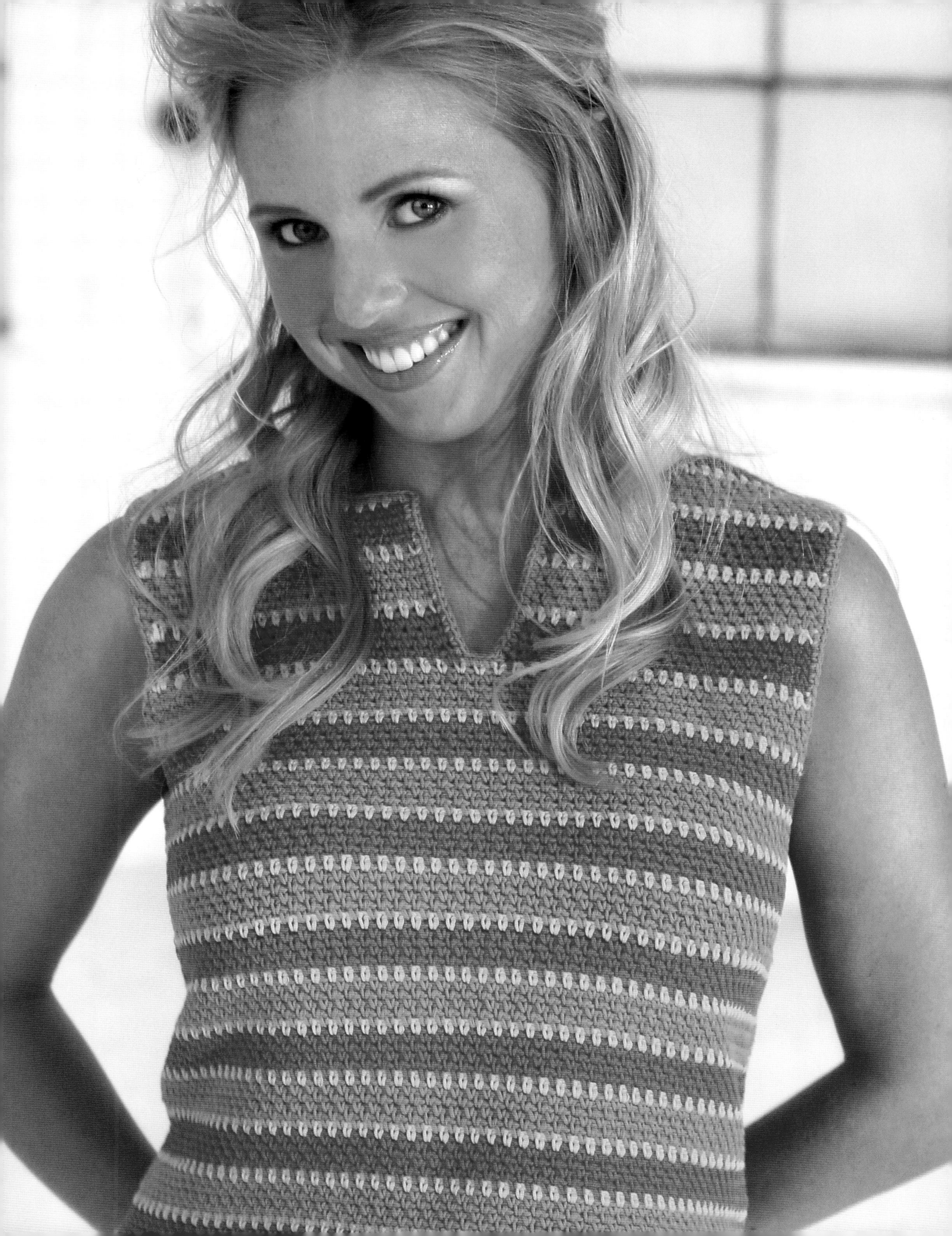

Darla

Made with stretchy, soft yarn and adjustable ties, this elegant wrap-top will fit you to a tee!

GAUGE

In Solid Hdc Patt, 22 sts and 14 rows = 4". To measure your gauge, make a test swatch as follows: Ch 23. Work Solid Hdc Patt on 22 sts for 14 rows total. Fasten off. Piece should measure 4" square. **To save time, take time to check gauge.**

SOLID HALF DOUBLE CROCHET PATTERN

(any number of sts)

Foundation Row (RS): Hdc into third ch from hook and into each ch across. Ch 2, turn.

Patt Row: Skip first hdc, *hdc into next hdc. Repeat from * across, ending row with hdc into top of turning-ch-2. Ch 2, turn.

Repeat Patt Row for patt.

NOTES

Throughout, each hdc, dec hdc, and turning-ch-2 counts as 1 st.

To increase 1 st each side, ch 2 to turn; skip first st, 2 hdc into next st; hdc into each st across until 2 sts rem, ending row with 2 hdc into next st, hdc into top of turning-ch-2. Ch 2, turn.

To decrease 1 st each side, ch 2 to turn; skip first st, work a dec hdc to combine next 2 sts; hdc into each st across until 3 sts rem, ending row with dec hdc to combine next 2 sts, hdc into top of turning-ch-2. Ch 2, turn.

Continued on next page.

BACK

Ch 81 (89, 97, 111, 119).

Beg Solid Hdc Patt, and work even on 80 (88, 96, 110, 118) sts for 18 (18, 14, 10, 10) rows. Ch 2, turn.

Shape Body

Inc 1 st each side on next row and then every sixth (sixth, sixth, eighth, eighth) row 3 more times—88 (96, 104, 118, 126) sts.

Cont even in patt as established until piece measures approx 13½" from beg, ending after WS row. *Do not ch 2.* Turn.

Shape Armholes

Next (RS): Slip st into first 4 (6, 7, 9, 9) sts, ch 2. Skip st where last slip st was worked, hdc into next st and into each st across until 3 (5, 6, 8, 8) sts rem—82 (86, 92, 102, 110) sts rem. Ch 2, turn, leaving rest of row unworked.

Dec 1 st each side every row 2 (2, 6, 12, 16) times, then every other row 4 (5, 4, 2, 1) times—70 (72, 72, 74, 76) sts rem.

Cont even until piece measures approx 20 (20¼, 20½, 21, 21½)" from beg, ending after WS row.

SKILL LEVEL
Advanced

SIZES
Small (Medium, Large, Extra-Large, Extra-Extra-Large). *Instructions are for smallest size, with changes for other sizes noted in parentheses as necessary.*

FINISHED MEASUREMENTS
Bust: 32 (35, 38, 43, 46)"
Total length: 21 (21¼, 21½, 22, 22½)"

MATERIALS
Classic Elite's *Star* (light worsted weight; 99% cotton/ 1% Lycra®; each approx 1¾ oz/50 g and 112 yd/ 102 m), 13 (14, 15, 16, 17) hanks Iris #5179

Crochet hook, size G/6 (4.00 mm) or size needed to obtain gauge

To decrease 2 sts each side, ch 2 to turn; skip first st, (work a dec hdc to combine next 2 sts) twice; hdc into each st across until 5 sts rem, ending row with (dec hdc to combine next 2 sts) twice, hdc into top of turning-ch-2. Ch 2, turn.

Decrease half double crochet = dec hdc = Yarn over hook, insert hook into next st and pull up a loop (3 loops are on your hook); yarn over hook, insert hook into next st and pull up a loop; yarn over hook and draw loop through all 5 loops on hook.

Decrease single crochet = dec sc = (Insert hook into next st and pull up a loop) twice, yarn over hook and draw loop through all 3 loops on hook.

For sweater assembly, refer to the illustration for set-in construction on page 126.

Shape Neck
Next Row (RS): Work across first 17 (18, 18, 19, 20) sts, ch 2, turn, leaving rest of row unworked.

Cont even in patt as established until this side measures approx 21 (21¼, 21½, 22, 22½)" from beg.

Fasten off.

For second side of neck, skip the middle 36 sts, and with RS facing, attach yarn with a slip st to next st and ch 2. Skip st where slip st was worked, work across to end row.

Complete same as first side.

LEFT FRONT
Ch 74 (81, 89, 102, 107).

Beg Solid Hdc Patt, and work even on 73 (80, 88, 101, 106) sts for 18 (18, 14, 10, 10) rows. Ch 2, turn.

Shape Body, Shape Armhole, and Shape Neck
Inc 1 st at beg of next row and then every sixth (sixth, sixth, eighth, eighth) row 3 more times; **and at the same time,** dec 1 st at neck edge every row 52 (54, 58, 64, 65) times; when piece measures 13½" from beg, ending after RS row, shape armhole same as for back—16 (18, 18, 19, 20) sts rem.

Cont even in patt as established until piece measures approx 21 (21¼ 21½, 22, 22½)" from beg.

Fasten off.

RIGHT FRONT
Ch 74 (81, 89, 102, 107).

Beg Solid Hdc Patt, and work even on 73 (80, 88, 101, 106) sts for 18 (18, 14, 10, 10) rows. Ch 2, turn.

Shape Body, Shape Armhole, and Shape Neck
Inc 1 st at end of next row and then every sixth (sixth, sixth, eighth, eighth) row 3 more times; **and at the same time,** dec 1 st at neck edge every row 52 (54, 58, 64, 65) times; when piece measures 13½" from beg, ending after RS row, shape armhole same as for back—16 (18, 18, 19, 20) sts rem.

Cont even in patt as established until piece measures approx 21 (21¼, 21½, 22, 22½)" from beg.

Fasten off.

SLEEVES

Ch 53.

Beg Solid Hdc Patt, and inc 1 st each side every row 0 (0, 0, 6, 12) times, every other row 7 (13, 15, 12, 9) times, then every fourth row 4 (1, 0, 0, 0) times—74 (80, 82, 88, 94) sts.

Cont even in patt as established until piece measures approx 10" from beg, ending after WS row. *Do not ch 2.* Turn.

Shape Cap
Next Row (RS): Slip st into first 4 (6, 7, 9, 9) sts, ch 2. Skip st where last slip st was worked, hdc into next st and into each st across until 3 (5, 6, 8, 8) sts rem—68 (70, 70, 72, 78) sts. Ch 2, turn, leaving rest of row unworked.

Dec 1 st each side every row 5 (8, 12, 15, 16) times—58 (54, 46, 42, 46) sts rem.

Dec 2 sts each side every row 9 (8, 6, 5, 6) times—22 sts rem. *Do not ch 2.* Turn.

Next Row: Slip st into first 3 sts, ch 2. Skip st where last slip st was worked, hdc into next st and into each st across until 2 sts rem—18 sts. *Do not ch 2.* Turn.

Next Row: Slip st into first 3 sts, ch 2. Skip st where last slip st was worked, hdc into next st and into each st across until 2 sts rem—14 sts.

Fasten off.

FINISHING

Sew shoulder seams. Set in sleeves. Sew sleeve seams.

Front Edging
With RS facing, attach yarn with a slip st to lower edge of right front and ch 1.

Work 2 rows of sc evenly spaced along right front edge, around back of neck, and along left front edge, working 2 sc at beg of each front neck shaping and working a dec sc at beg of each back neck shaping.

Fasten off.

Left Tie
Ch 247.

Slip st into each ch across.

Fasten off.

Attach tie to left front at beg of neck shaping.

Right Tie
Ch 225.

Slip st into each ch across.

Fasten off.

Attach tie to right front at beg of neck shaping.

Sew side seams, leaving ½" unsewn for tie opening on right side, approx 5 (5, 4, 3, 3)" from lower edge.

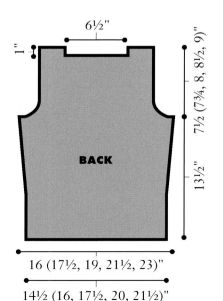

BACK

6½"

1"

7½ (7¾, 8, 8½, 9)"

13½"

16 (17½, 19, 21½, 23)"

14½ (16, 17½, 20, 21½)"

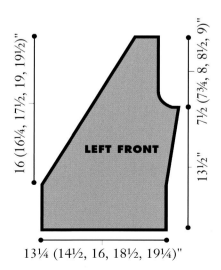

LEFT FRONT

16 (16¼, 17½, 19, 19½)"

7½ (7¾, 8, 8½, 9)"

13½"

13¼ (14½, 16, 18½, 19¼)"

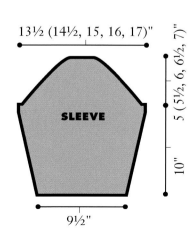

SLEEVE

13½ (14½, 15, 16, 17)"

5 (5½, 6, 6½, 7)"

10"

9½"

Julianna

Searching for a ladylike cardigan with the look of vintage lace? This design features a sleek silhouette, ¾-length sleeves, and fun-to-make crocheted buttons.

GAUGE

In Lace Patt, with larger hook, 28 sts and 14 rows = 4". To measure your gauge, make a test swatch as follows: With larger hook, ch 31. Work Lace Patt on 30 sts for 16 rows total. Fasten off. Piece should measure 4¼" wide and 4½" high. **To save time, take time to check gauge.**

LACE PATTERN
(mult 6 sts)

Foundation Row (RS): Sc into second ch from hook, *ch 5, skip next 4 ch, sc into next 2 ch. Repeat from * across, ending row with ch 5, skip next 4 ch, sc into last ch. Ch 5, turn.

Row 1 (WS): *Sc into next ch-5 sp, ch 2, dc into next 2 sc, ch 2. Repeat from * across, ending row with sc into next ch-5 sp, ch 2, dc into last sc. Ch 6, turn.

Row 2: *Sc into next sc, ch 3, dc into next 2 dc, ch 3. Repeat from * across, ending row with sc into next sc, ch 3, dc into third ch of turning-ch-5. Ch 1, turn.

Row 3: Sc into first dc, *ch 4, sc into next 2 dc. Repeat from * across, ending row with ch 4, sc into third ch of turning-ch-6. Ch 1, turn.

Row 4: Sc into first sc, *ch 5, sc into next 2 sc. Repeat from * across, ending row with ch 5, sc into last sc. Ch 5, turn.

Repeat Rows 1-4 for patt.

Continued on next page.

BACK

With larger hook, ch 121 (133, 145, 157, 169).

Beg Lace Patt, and work even on 120 (132, 144, 156, 168) sts until piece measures approx 12½" from beg, ending after Row 3 of patt. *Do not ch 1.* Turn.

Shape Armholes

Decrease Row 1 (RS): Slip st into first 7 (13, 13, 19, 19) sts, ch 1, sc into same sc as slip st, *ch 5, sc into next 2 sc. Repeat from * across until 6 (12, 12, 18, 18) sts rem in row. Ch 3, turn, leaving rest of row unworked.

Decrease Row 2: Sc into ch-5 sp, *ch 2, dc into next 2 sc, ch 2, sc into next ch-5 sp. Repeat from * across, ending row with dc into last sc. Ch 4, turn.

Decrease Row 3: *Dc into next 2 dc, ch 3, sc into next sc, ch 3. Repeat from * across, ending row with dc into next 2 dc, tr into top of turning-ch-3. Ch 1, turn.

Decrease Row 4: Dec sc to combine first tr and second dc, *ch 4, sc into next 2 dc. Repeat from * across, ending row with ch 4, dec sc to combine next dc and turning-ch-4. Ch 1, turn.

SKILL LEVEL
Advanced

SIZES
Small (Medium, Large, Extra-Large, Extra-Extra-Large). *Instructions are for smallest size, with changes for other sizes noted in parentheses as necessary.*

FINISHED MEASUREMENTS
Bust (buttoned): 34 (38, 41, 44½, 48)"
Total length: 20 (20, 21, 21, 21)"

MATERIALS
Muench Yarn's *Scarlett* (sport weight; 100% mercerized Egyptian cotton; each approx 1¾ oz/50 g and 121 yd/111 m), 11 (12, 13, 14, 15) balls Raspberry #09

Crochet hooks, sizes D/3 and E/4 (3.25 and 3.50 mm) or size needed to obtain gauge

NOTES

To count the number of sts across your fabric, do so *only* immediately after working Row 3 of Lace Patt: Each sc counts as 1 st; each ch-4 counts as 4 sts.

Decrease single crochet = dec sc = (Insert hook into next st and pull up a loop) twice, yarn over hook and draw loop through all 3 loops on hook.

For sweater assembly, refer to the illustration for set-in construction on page 126.

Decrease Row 5: Sc into first st, *ch 5, sc into next 2 sc. Repeat from * across, ending row with ch 5, sc into last st. Ch 3, turn.

Repeat Armhole Decrease Rows 2-5 once (once, once, once, twice) more. After last repeat, ch 5 instead of ch 3 to turn.

Beg with Row 1 of patt, cont even on 84 (84, 96, 96, 96) sts in patt as established until piece measures approx 19 (19, 20, 20, 20)" from beg, ending after Row 3 of patt. Ch 1, turn.

Shape Neck
Next Row (RS): Sc into first sc, *ch 5, sc into next 2 sc. Repeat from * once (once, twice, twice, twice) more, ch 5, sc into next sc. Ch 5, turn, leaving rest of row unworked.

Beg with Row 1 of patt, cont even in patt as established until this side measures approx 20 (20, 21, 21, 21)" from beg, ending after Row 3 of patt—18 (18, 24, 24, 24) sts rem on this side.

Fasten off.

For second side of neck, with RS facing and larger hook, skip the middle 48 sts, and attach yarn with a slip st to next st and ch 1. Complete same as first side.

Fasten off.

LEFT FRONT

With larger hook, ch 61 (67, 73, 79, 85).

Beg Lace Patt, and work even on 60 (66, 72, 78, 84) sts until piece measures approx 12½" from beg, ending after Row 3 of patt. *Do not ch 1.* Turn.

Shape Armhole
Decrease Row 1 (RS): Slip st into first 7 (13, 13, 19, 19) sts, ch 1, sc into same sc as slip st, *ch 5, sc into next 2 sc. Repeat from * across, ending row with ch 5, sc into last sc. Ch 5, turn.

Decrease Row 2: *Sc into next ch-5 sp, ch 2, dc into next 2 sc, ch 2. Repeat from * across, ending row with sc into next ch-5 sp, dc into last sc. Ch 4, turn.

Decrease Row 3: *Dc into next 2 dc, ch 3, sc into next sc, ch 3. Repeat from * across, ending row with dc into third ch of turning-ch-5. Ch 1, turn.

Decrease Row 4: Sc into first dc, *ch 4, sc into next 2 dc. Repeat from * across, ending row with ch 4, dec sc to combine next dc and turning-ch-4. Ch 1, turn.

Decrease Row 5: Sc into first st, *ch 5, sc into next 2 sc. Repeat from * across, ending row with ch 5, sc into last st. Ch 5, turn.

Repeat Armhole Decrease Rows 2-5 once (once, once, once, twice) more. After last repeat, ch 5 instead of ch 3 to turn.

Beg with Row 1 of patt, cont even on 42 (42, 48, 48, 48) sts in patt as established until piece measures approx 15½ (15½, 16½, 16½, 16½)" from beg, ending after Row 4 of patt. Ch 3, turn.

Shape Neck
Decrease Row 1 (WS): *Sc into next ch-5 sp, ch 2, dc into next 2 sc, ch 2. Repeat from * across, ending row with sc into next ch-5 sp, ch 2, dc into last sc. Ch 6, turn.

Decrease Row 2: *Sc into next sc, ch 3, dc into next 2 dc, ch 3. Repeat from * across, ending row with sc into next sc, ch 3, dc into next 2 dc, tr into top of turning-ch-3. Ch 1, turn.

Decrease Row 3: Dec sc to combine tr and first dc, sc into next dc, *ch 4, sc into next 2 dc. Repeat from * across, ending row with ch 4, sc into third ch of turning-ch-6. Ch 1, turn.

Decrease Row 4: Sc into first sc, *ch 5, sc into next 2 sc. Repeat from * across, ending row with ch 5, dec sc to combine last 2 sts. Ch 3, turn.

Repeat Neck Decrease Rows 1-4 3 more times—18 (18, 24, 24, 24) sts rem.

Cont even, if necessary, in patt as established until piece measures same as back to shoulders.

Fasten off.

RIGHT FRONT

Same as left front until piece measures same as left front to armhole, ending after Row 3 of patt. Ch 1, turn.

Shape Armhole

Decrease Row 1 (RS): Sc into first sc, *ch 5, sc into next 2 sc. Repeat from * across until 6 (12, 12, 18, 18) sts rem in row. Ch 3, turn, leaving rest of row unworked.

Decrease Row 2: Sc into ch-5 sp, *ch 2, dc into next 2 sc, ch 2, sc into next ch-5 sp. Repeat from * across, ending row with dc into last sc. Ch 6, turn.

Decrease Row 3: *Sc into next sc, ch 3, dc into next 2 dc, ch 3. Repeat from * across, ending row with sc into next sc, ch 3, dc into next 2 dc, tr into top of turning-ch-3. Ch 1, turn.

Decrease Row 4: Dec sc to combine first tr and second dc, *ch 4, sc into next 2 dc. Repeat from * across, ending row with ch 4, sc into third ch of turning-ch-6. Ch 1, turn.

Decrease Row 5: Sc into first st, *ch 5, sc into next 2 sc. Repeat from * across, ending row with ch 5, sc into last st. Ch 3, turn.

Repeat Armhole Decrease Rows 2-5 once (once, once, once, twice) more. After last repeat, ch 5 instead of ch 3 to turn.

Beg with Row 1 of patt, cont even on 42 (42, 48, 48, 48) sts in patt as established until piece measures approx 15½ (15½, 16½, 16½ 16½)" from beg, ending after Row 4 of patt. Ch 5, turn.

Shape Neck

Decrease Row 1 (WS): *Sc into next ch-5 sp, ch 2, dc into next 2 sc, ch 2. Repeat from * across, ending row with sc into next ch-5 sp, dc into last sc. Ch 4, turn.

Decrease Row 2: Skip first dc and sc, *dc into next 2 dc, ch 3, sc into next sc, ch 2. Repeat from * across, ending row with dc into third ch of turning-ch-5. Ch 1, turn.

Decrease Row 3: Sc into first dc, *ch 4, sc into next 2 dc. Repeat from * across, ending row with ch 4, sc into next dc, dec sc to combine next dc and top of turning-ch-4. Ch 1, turn.

Decrease Row 4: Dec sc to combine first 2 sts, *ch 5, sc into next 2 sc. Repeat from * across, ending row with ch 5, sc into last sc. Ch 5, turn.

Repeat Neck Decrease Rows 1-4 3 more times— 18 (18, 24, 24, 24) sts rem.

Complete same as left front.

SLEEVES

With larger hook, ch 73 (73, 85, 85, 85).

Beg Lace Patt, and work even on 72 (72, 84, 84, 84) sts until piece measures approx 2¼" from beg, ending after Row 4 of patt. Ch 3 instead of ch 5, turn.

Next Row (WS): Dc into first sc, *ch 2, sc into next ch-5 sp, ch 2, dc into next 2 sc. Repeat from * across, ending row with ch 2, sc into next ch-5 sp, ch 2, 2 dc into last sc. Ch 3, turn.

Next Row: Skip first dc, dc into next dc, *ch 3, sc into next sc, ch 3, dc into next 2 dc. Repeat from * across, ending row with ch 3, sc into next sc, ch 3, dc into next dc, dc into top of turning-ch-3. Ch 1, turn.

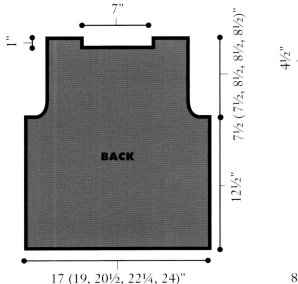

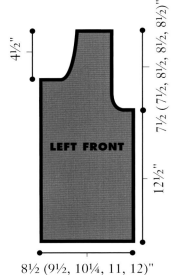

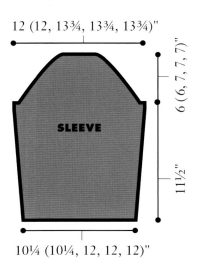

Note: Measurements in schematic drawings do not include lower edging.

Next Row: Sc into first 2 dc, *ch 4, sc into next 2 dc. Repeat from * across, ending row with ch 4, sc into next dc, sc into top of turning-ch-3. Ch 1, turn.

Next Row: Sc into first 2 sc, *ch 5, sc into next 2 sc. Repeat from * across. Ch 3, turn.

Next Row: Dc into first sc, dc into next sc, *ch 2, sc into next ch-5 sp, ch 2, dc into next 2 sc. Repeat from * across, ending row with ch 2, sc into next ch-5 sp, ch 2, dc into next sc, 2 dc into last sc. Ch 3, turn.

Next Row: Skip first dc, dc into next 2 dc, *ch 3, sc into next sc, ch 3, dc into next 2 dc. Repeat from * across, ending row with dc into top of turning-ch-3. Ch 1, turn.

Next Row: Sc into first 3 dc, *ch 4, sc into next 2 dc. Repeat from * across, ending row with sc into top of turning-ch-3. Ch 3, turn.

Next Row: Skip first sc, *sc into next 2 sc, ch 5. Repeat from * across, ending row with sc into next 2 sc, ch 1, hdc into last sc. Ch 3, turn.

Next Row: *Dc into next 2 sc, ch 2, sc into next ch-5 sp, ch 2. Repeat from * across, ending row with dc into next 2 sc, ch 1, hdc into second ch of turning-ch-3. Ch 1, turn.

Next Row: Sc into hdc, ch 2, *dc into next 2 dc, ch 3, sc into next sc, ch 3. Repeat from * across, ending row with dc into next 2 dc, ch 2, sc into second ch of turning-ch-3. Ch 5, turn.

Next Row: *Sc into next 2 dc, ch 4. Repeat from * across, ending row with sc into next 2 dc, ch 2, dc into last sc. Ch 5, turn.

Next Row: *Sc into next 2 sc, ch 5. Repeat from * across, ending row with sc into next 2 sc, ch 2, dc into third ch of turning-ch-5. Ch 1, turn.

Next Row: Sc into first dc, sc into next ch-2 sp, *ch 2, dc into next 2 sc, ch 2, sc into next ch-5 sp. Repeat from * across, ending row with ch 2, dc into next 2 sc, ch 2, sc into next ch-5 sp, sc into third ch of turning-ch-5. Ch 6, turn.

Next Row: Skip first sc, sc into next sc, *ch 3, dc into next 2 dc, ch 3, sc into next sc. Repeat from * across, ending row with ch 3, dc into next 2 dc, ch 3, sc into next sc, ch 3, dc into last sc. Ch 1, turn.

Next Row: Sc into first dc, ch 3, *sc into next 2 dc, ch 4. Repeat from * across, ending row with sc into next 2 dc, ch 3, sc into third ch of turning-ch-6. Ch 1, turn.

Next Row: Sc into first sc, ch 4, *sc into next 2 sc, ch 5. Repeat from * across, ending row with sc into next 2 sc, ch 4, sc into last sc. Ch 4, turn.

Next Row: Sc into ch-4 sp, *ch 2, dc into next 2 sc, ch 2, sc into next ch-5 sp. Repeat from * across, ending row with ch 2, dc into next 2 sc, ch 2, sc into next ch-4 sp, ch 1, dc into last sc. Ch 6, turn.

Next Row: *Sc into next sc, ch 3, dc into next 2 dc, ch 3. Repeat from * across, ending row with sc into next sc, ch 3, dc into third ch of turning-ch-4. Ch 1, turn.

Next Row: Sc into first dc, *ch 4, sc into next 2 dc. Repeat from * across, ending row with ch 4, sc into third ch of turning-ch-6. Ch 1, turn.

Next Row: Sc into first sc, *ch 5, sc into next 2 sc. Repeat from * across, ending row with ch 5, sc into last sc. Ch 5, turn.

Beg with Row 1 of patt, cont even on 84 (84, 96, 96, 96) sts in patt as established until piece measures approx 11½" from beg, ending after Row 3 of patt. *Do not ch 1.* Turn.

Shape Cap
Decrease Row 1 (RS): Slip st into first 7 (13, 13, 19, 19) sts, ch 1, sc into same sc as slip st, *ch 5, sc into next 2 sc. Repeat from * across until 6 (12, 12, 18, 18) sts rem in row. Ch 3, turn, leaving rest of row unworked.

Decrease Row 2: Sc into ch-5 sp, *ch 2, dc into next 2 sc, ch 2, sc into next ch-5 sp. Repeat from * across, ending row with dc into last sc. Ch 4, turn.

Decrease Row 3: *Dc into next 2 dc, ch 3, sc into next sc, ch 3. Repeat from * across, ending row with dc into next 2 dc, tr into top of turning-ch-3. Ch 1, turn.

Decrease Row 4: Dec sc to combine first tr and second dc, *ch 4, sc into next 2 dc. Repeat from * across, ending row with ch 4, dec sc to combine next dc and turning-ch-4. Ch 1, turn.

Decrease Row 5: Sc into first st, *ch 5, sc into next 2 sc. Repeat from * across, ending row with ch 5, sc into last st. Ch 3, turn.

Cont even in patt as established for 0 (0, 4, 4, 4) rows.

Repeat Sleeve Cap Decrease Rows 2-5 4 (2, 4, 2, 2) more times—12 (24, 12, 24, 24) sts rem.

Cont even in patt as established for 0 (0, 4, 4, 4) rows.

Work Sleeve Cap Decrease Rows 2-5 0 (1, 0, 1, 1) more times—12 sts rem.

Fasten off.

FINISHING

Sew shoulder seams.

Set in sleeves. Sew sleeve and side seams.

Edging

With RS facing and smaller hook, attach yarn with a slip st to lower right side seam and ch 1.

Rnd 1 (RS): Work sc evenly spaced along lower right front edge, up right front, around back of neck, down left front, along lower left front edge, and around lower back edge, working 3 sc at lower front corners and at beg of both front neck shapings. Join with a slip st to first sc. Ch 1.

Place markers for 3 evenly spaced buttonholes on right front, making the first ⅛" from beg of neck shaping and the last 5" from lower edge.

Rnd 2: Same as Rnd 1, making 3 buttonholes where marked as follows: (ch 4, skip next 4 sc). Join with a slip st to first sc. Ch 1.

Rnd 3: Same as Rnd 1, working 4 sc into each ch-4 sp of Rnd 2. Join with a slip st to first sc.

Fasten off.

Buttons *(Make 3)*
With smaller hook, ch 4. Join with a slip st to form a ring. Ch 1.

Rnd 1: 6 sc into ring. Join with a slip st to first sc. Ch 1.

Rnd 2: 2 sc into same st as slip st, *2 sc into next sc. Repeat from * around, ending rnd with a slip st to first sc—12 sc. Ch 1.

Rnd 3: Sc into same st as slip st, *sc into next sc. Repeat from * around, ending rnd with a slip st to first sc—12 sc. Ch 1.

Rnd 4: Sc into same st as slip st, *dec sc to combine next 2 sc, sc into next sc. Repeat from * around, ending rnd with dec sc to combine next 2 sc, join with a slip st to first sc—8 sc rem.

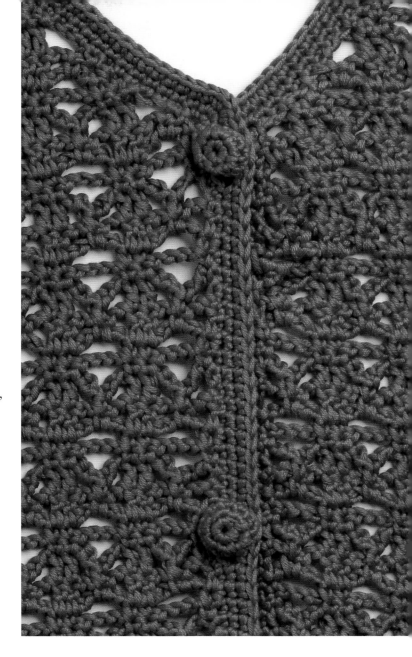

Fasten off, leaving 6" tail.

Thread yarn tail through loops of last rnd and pull to tighten.

Fasten off.

Sew on buttons opposite markers.

Lower Sleeve Edging
With RS facing and smaller hook, attach yarn with a slip st to lower sleeve seam and ch 1.

Rnd 1 (RS): Work sc evenly spaced around cuff. Join with a slip st to first sc. Ch 1.

Rnd 2: Same as Rnd 1.

Rnd 3: Same as Rnd 1.

Fasten off.

Valentina

Wrap yourself in luxury! This airy stole is made out of the softest yarn imaginable—a brushed baby alpaca blend.

GAUGE

In Openwork Patt, with larger hook, 10 sts and 6 rows = 4". To measure your gauge, make a test swatch as follows: Ch 18. Work Openwork Patt for 8 rows total. Fasten off. Piece should measure 6¾" wide and 5¼" high. **To save time, take time to check gauge.**

OPENWORK PATTERN

Foundation Row (RS): Sc into second ch from hook, *ch 5, skip next 3 ch, sc into next ch. Repeat from * across. Ch 6, turn.

Row 1 (WS): *Sc into next ch-5 sp, (dc, ch 1, dc, ch 1, dc) into next sc, sc into next ch-5 sp, ch 6, skip next sc. Repeat from * across, ending row with sc into next ch-5 sp, (dc, ch 1, dc, ch 1, dc) into next sc, sc into next ch-5 sp, ch 3, dc into last sc. Ch 1, turn.

Row 2: Sc into first dc, *(dc, ch 1, dc, ch 1, dc) into next sc, skip next dc, skip next ch-1 sp, sc into next dc, skip next ch-1 sp, skip next dc, (dc, ch 1, dc, ch 1, dc) into next sc, sc into next ch 6-sp. Repeat from * across, ending row with (dc, ch 1, dc, ch 1, dc) into next sc, skip next dc, skip next ch-1 sp, sc into next dc, skip next ch-1 sp, skip next dc, (dc, ch 1, dc, ch 1, dc) into next sc, sc under turning-ch-6. Ch 5, turn.

Continued on next page.

STOLE

With larger hook, ch 154.

Beg Openwork Patt, and work even until piece measures approx 21¼" from beg, ending after Row 3 of patt.

Next Row (RS): Sc into first dc, ch 3, skip next ch-2 sp, *skip next sc, skip next dc, skip next ch-1 sp, sc into next dc, ch 3, skip next ch-1 sp, skip next dc, skip next sc, sc into next ch-5 sp, ch 3. Repeat from * across, ending row with skip next sc, skip next dc, skip next ch-1 sp, sc into next dc, ch 3, skip next ch-1 sp, skip next dc, skip next sc, sc into next ch-5 sp. *Do not ch 6. Do not fasten off.*

FINISHING

Edging

With RS facing, change to smaller hook and ch 1.

SKILL LEVEL
Advanced Beginner

SIZES
One size

FINISHED MEASUREMENTS
Approx 21¼" wide and 61" long (excluding edging)

MATERIALS
Plymouth's *Baby Alpaca Brush* (bulky weight; 80% baby alpaca/20% acrylic; each approx ⅞ oz/25 g and 110 yd/101 m), 8 balls Periwinkle Twist #109

Crochet hooks, sizes I/9 and K/10.5 (5.50 and 6.50 mm) or size needed to obtain gauge

Row 3: Skip first sc, *skip next dc, skip next ch-1 sp, sc into next dc, skip next ch-1 sp, skip next dc, (dc, ch 1, dc, ch 1, dc) into next sc, skip next dc, skip next ch-1 sp, sc into next dc, ch 5, skip next ch-1 sp, skip next dc, skip next sc. Repeat from * across, ending row with skip next dc, skip next ch-1 sp, sc into next dc, skip next ch-1 sp, skip next dc, (dc, ch 1, dc, ch 1, dc) into next sc, skip next dc, skip next ch-1 sp, sc into next dc, ch 2, dc into last sc. Ch 1, turn.

Row 4: Sc into first dc, ch 5, skip next ch-2 sp, *skip next sc, skip next dc, skip next ch-1 sp, sc into next dc, ch 5, skip next ch-1 sp, skip next dc, skip next sc, sc into next ch-5 sp, ch 5. Repeat from * across, ending row with skip next sc, skip next dc, skip next ch-1 sp, sc into next dc, ch 5, skip next ch-1 sp, skip next dc, skip next sc, sc into next ch-5 sp. Ch 6, turn.

Repeat Rows 1-4 for patt.

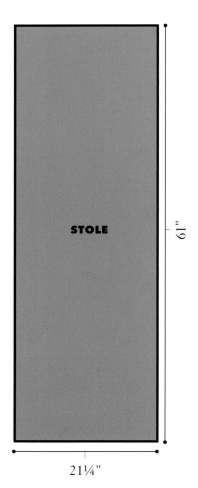

STOLE

61"

21¼"

Note: Measurements in schematic drawing do not include edging.

Rnd 1 (RS): Sc into last sc of last row, and working along side edge of stole, *ch 5, sc into side of next sc. Repeat from * across to next corner; ch 5, work (sc, ch 2, sc) into corner; working into unused loops of foundation chain, **ch 5, sc into same ch as next sc. Repeat from ** across to next corner; ch 5, work (sc, ch 2, sc) into corner; ***ch 5, sc into side of next sc. Repeat from *** across to next corner; ch 5, work (sc, ch 2, sc) into corner; ****ch 5, sc into next sc. Repeat from **** across to next corner, ch 5, sc into same sc as first sc, ch 2, join with a slip st to first sc.

Rnd 2: Slip st into next ch-5 sp, *3 dc into next sc, slip st into next ch-5 sp. Repeat from * across to next corner; work 7 dc into corner ch-2 sp, sc into next ch-5 sp, **5 dc into next sc, sc into next ch-5 sp. Repeat from ** across to next corner; work 7 dc into corner ch-2 sp, slip st into next ch-5 sp. Repeat from * once more, ending rnd with a slip st to first slip st.

Fasten off.

Penina

Toss this versatile jacket over any outfit and you're good to go!
Its beautiful openwork fabric drapes elegantly.

GAUGE

In Open Lattice Patt, with larger hook, each (dc, ch 5, dc) measures ¾" wide and 10 rows = 4". To measure your gauge, make a test swatch as follows: With larger hook, ch 26. Work Open Lattice Patt for 10 rows total. Fasten off. Piece should measure 4" square. **To save time, take time to check gauge.**

OPEN LATTICE PATTERN

Foundation Row 1 (WS): Sc into second ch from hook and into next ch, *ch 5, skip next 3 ch, sc into next 3 ch. Repeat from * across, ending row with ch 5, skip next 3 ch, sc into last 2 ch. Ch 5, turn.

Foundation Row 2: Dc into first sc, *sc into next ch-5 sp, skip next sc, (dc, ch 5, dc) into next sc. Repeat from * across, ending row with sc into next ch-5 sp, skip next sc, (dc, ch 2, dc) into last sc. Ch 1, turn.

Row 1 (WS): Sc into first dc, *(dc, ch 5, dc) into next sc, sc into next ch-5 sp. Repeat from * across, ending row with (dc, ch 5, dc) into next sc, sc into third ch of turning-ch-5. Ch 5, turn.

Row 2: Dc into first sc, *sc into next ch-5 sp, (dc, ch 5, dc) into next sc. Repeat from * across, ending row with sc into next ch-5 sp, (dc, ch 2, dc) into last sc. Ch 1, turn.

Repeat Rows 1 and 2 for patt.

Continued on next page.

BACK

With larger hook, ch 110 (122, 146, 158, 182).

Beg Open Lattice Patt, and work even until piece measures approx 9½" from beg, ending after RS Row. Ch 1, turn.

Shape Armholes
Next Row (WS): Sc into first dc, [(dc, ch 2, dc) into next sc, sc into next ch-5-sp] 3 (3, 5, 6, 7) times, [(dc, ch 5, dc) into next sc, sc into next ch-5-sp] 12 (14, 14, 14, 16) times, [(dc, ch 2, dc) into next sc, sc into next ch-5 sp] 2 (2, 4, 5, 6) times, ending row with (dc, ch 2, dc) into next sc, sc into third ch of turning-ch-5. *Do not ch 5.* Turn.

Next Row: Slip st into first 16 (16, 26, 31, 36) sts, ch 5, dc into same sc as last slip st, [sc into next ch-5 sp, (dc, ch 5, dc) into next sc] 11 (13, 13, 13, 15) times, sc into next ch-5 sp, (dc, ch 2, dc) into next sc. Ch 1, turn, leaving rest of row unworked.

Beg with Row 1 of patt, cont even in patt as established until piece measures approx 16½, (17, 17, 17½, 17½)" from beg, ending after RS row. Ch 1, turn.

SKILL LEVEL
Advanced

SIZES
Small (Medium, Large, Extra-Large, Extra-Extra-Large).
Instructions are for smallest size, with changes for other sizes noted in parentheses as necessary.

FINISHED MEASUREMENTS
Bust: 36 (40, 47, 52, 60)"
Total length (excluding edging): 18 (18½, 18½, 19, 19)"

MATERIALS
Dale of Norway's *Tuir* (sport weight; 60% mohair/ 40% wool; each approx 1¾ oz/50 g and 126 yd/ 115 m), 9 (10, 11, 12, 13) balls Magenta #4545

Crochet hooks, sizes F/5 and G/6 (3.75 and 4.00 mm) or size needed to obtain gauge

REVERSE SINGLE CROCHET PATTERN
(any number of sts)
Patt Rnd (RS): Working from left to right, sc into each st around.

NOTES
When working slip stitches at armhole shaping, each dc, ch, and sc counts as 1 st.

For sweater assembly, refer to the illustration for square indented construction on page 126.

Shape Neck
Next Row (WS): Sc into first dc, [(dc, ch 5, dc) into next sc, sc into next ch-5 sp] 3 (4, 4, 4, 5) times, [(dc, ch 2, dc) into next sc, sc into next ch-5 sp] 6 times, [(dc, ch 5, dc) into next sc, sc into next ch-5 sp] 3 (4, 4, 4, 5) times, (dc, ch 5, dc) into next sc, sc into third ch of turning-ch. Ch 5, turn.

Next Row (RS): Dc into first sc, [sc into next ch-5 sp, (dc, ch 5, dc) into next sc] 2 (3, 3, 3, 4) times, sc into next ch-5 sp, (dc, ch 2, dc) into next sc. Ch 1, turn, leaving rest of row unworked.

Cont even, if necessary, in patt as established until this side measures approx 17½ (18, 18, 18½, 18½)" from beg, ending after RS row. Ch 1, turn.

Next Row (WS): Sc into first dc, *(dc, ch 2, dc) into next sc, sc into next ch-5 sp. Repeat from * across, ending row with (dc, ch 2, dc) into next sc, sc into third ch of turning-ch-5.

Fasten off.

For second side of neck, with RS facing and larger hook, skip the middle 6 ch-2 spaces, attach yarn with a slip st to next sc and ch 5.

Complete same as first side.

Fasten off.

LEFT FRONT
With larger hook, ch 32 (38, 50, 56, 68).

Work Foundation Row of Open Lattice Patt. Ch 5, turn.

Shape Lower Front Curve
Next Row (RS): Dc into first sc, *sc into next ch-5 sp, skip next sc, (dc, ch 5, dc) into next sc. Repeat from * across, ending row with sc into next ch-5 sp, skip next sc, (dc, ch 5, dc) into last sc. Ch 5, turn.

Next Row: Dc into first dc, *sc into next ch-5 sp, (dc, ch 5, dc) into next sc. Repeat from * across, ending row with sc into third ch of turning-ch-5. Ch 5, turn.

Next Row: Dc into first dc, *sc into next ch-5 sp, (dc, ch 5, dc) into next sc. Repeat from * across, ending row with sc under turning-ch, ch 2, dc into third ch of turning-ch-5. Ch 1, turn.

Next Row: Sc into first dc, *(dc, ch 5, dc) into next sc, sc into next ch-5 sp. Repeat from * across, ending row with (dc, ch 5, dc) into next sc, sc under turning-ch. Ch 5, turn.

Next Row: Dc into first sc, *sc into next ch-5 sp, (dc, ch 5, dc) into next sc. Repeat from * across, ending row with sc into next ch-5 sp, (dc, ch 5, dc) into last sc. Ch 5, turn.

Repeat last 4 rows once more. Ch 5, turn.

Next Row: Dc into first dc, *sc into next ch-5 sp, (dc, ch 5, dc) into next sc. Repeat from * across, ending row with sc into third ch of turning-ch-5. Ch 5, turn.

Next Row: Dc into first dc, *sc into next ch-5 sp, (dc, ch 5, dc) into next sc. Repeat from * across, ending row with sc under turning-ch, ch 2, dc into third ch of turning-ch. Ch 1, turn.

Next Row: Sc into first dc, *(dc, ch 5, dc) into next sc, sc into next ch-5 sp. Repeat from * across, ending row with (dc, ch 5, dc) into next sc, sc under turning-ch. Ch 5, turn.

Beg with Row 2 of patt, cont even in patt as established until piece measures approx 9½" from beg, ending after RS row. Ch 1, turn.

Shape Armhole
Next Row (WS): Sc into first dc, [(dc, ch 5, dc) into next sc, sc into next ch-5-sp] 5 (6, 8, 9, 11) times, [(dc, ch 2, dc) into next sc, sc into next ch-5-sp] twice, (dc, ch 2, dc) into next sc, sc into third ch of turning-ch. *Do not ch 5.* Turn.

Next Row: Slip st into first 16 (16, 26, 31, 36) sts, ch 5, dc into same sc as last slip st, *sc into next ch-5 sp, (dc, ch 5, dc) into next sc. Repeat from * across, ending row with sc into next ch-5 sp, (dc, ch 2, dc) into last sc. Ch 1, turn.

Beg with Row 1 of patt, cont even in patt as established until piece measures approx 14¾" from beg, ending after WS row. Ch 5, turn.

Shape Neck
Next Row (RS): Dc into first sc, [sc into next ch-5 sp, (dc, ch 5, dc) into next sc] 4 (5, 5, 5, 6) times, sc into next ch-5 sp, dc into last sc. Ch 3, turn.

COOL TIP For a longer version, simply add extra rows before working the armhole shaping.

Next Row: Skip first dc, skip next sc, *sc into next ch-5 sp, (dc, ch 5, dc) into next sc. Repeat from * across, ending row with sc into third ch of turning-ch-5. Ch 5, turn.

Next Row: Dc into first sc, [sc into next ch-5 sp, (dc, ch 5, dc) into next sc] 3 (4, 4, 4, 5) times, sc into next ch-5 sp, dc into next sc, ch 2, dc into top of turning-ch-3. Ch 1, turn.

Next Row: Sc into first dc, *(dc, ch 5, dc) into next sc, sc into next ch-5 sp. Repeat from * across, ending row with (dc, ch 5, dc) into next sc, sc into third ch of turning-ch-5. Ch 5, turn.

Next Row: Dc into first sc, [sc into next ch-5 sp, (dc, ch 5, dc) into next sc] 3 (4, 4, 4, 5) times, sc into next ch-5 sp, dc into last sc. Ch 3, turn.

Next Row: Skip first dc, skip next sc, *sc into next ch-5 sp, (dc, ch 5, dc) into next sc. Repeat from * across, ending row with sc into third ch of turning-ch-5. Ch 5, turn.

Next Row: Dc into first sc, [sc into next ch-5 sp, (dc, ch 5, dc) into next sc] 2 (3, 3, 3, 4) times, sc into next ch-5 sp, dc into next sc, ch 2, dc into top of turning-ch-3. Ch 1, turn.

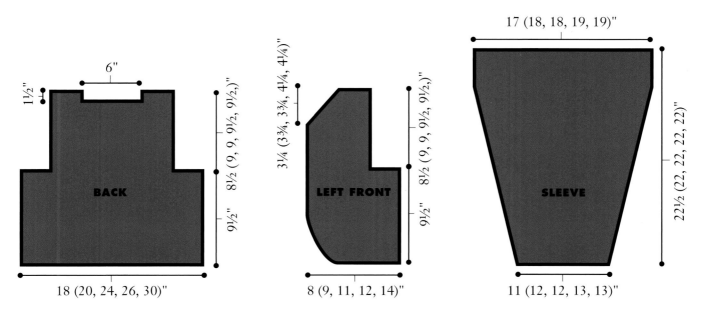

Note: Measurements in schematic drawings do not include lower edging.

Next Row: Sc into first dc, *(dc, ch 5, dc) into next sc, sc into next ch-5 sp. Repeat from * across, ending row with (dc, ch 5, dc) into next sc, sc into third ch of turning-ch-5. Ch 5, turn.

Cont even, if necessary, in patt as established until this side measures approx 17½ (18, 18, 18½, 18½)" from beg, ending after RS row. Ch 1, turn.

Next Row (WS): Sc into first dc, *(dc, ch 2, dc) into next sc, sc into next ch-5 sp. Repeat from * across, ending row with (dc, ch 2, dc) into next sc, sc into third ch of turning-ch-5.

Fasten off.

RIGHT FRONT

Same as left front, except RS and WS are reversed.

SLEEVES

With larger hook, ch 68 (74, 74, 80, 80).

Work Foundation Rows 1 and 2 of Open Lattice Patt. Ch 1, turn.

Next Row (WS): Sc into first dc, *(dc, ch 5, dc) into next sc, sc into next ch-5 sp. Repeat from * across, ending row with (dc, ch 5, dc) into next sc, sc into third ch of turning-ch-5. Ch 8, turn.

Next Row: Dc into first sc, *sc into next ch-5 sp, (dc, ch 5, dc) into next sc. Repeat from * across, ending row with sc into next ch-5 sp, (dc, ch 5, dc) into last sc. Ch 5, turn.

Next Row: Dc into first dc, *sc into next ch-5 sp, (dc, ch 5, dc) into next sc. Repeat from * across, ending row with sc under turning-ch, (dc, ch 2, dc) into third ch of turning-ch-8. Ch 1, turn.

Next Row: Sc into first dc, *(dc, ch 5, dc) into next sc, sc into next ch-5 sp. Repeat from * across, ending row with (dc, ch 5, dc) into next sc, sc into third ch of turning-ch-5. Ch 5, turn.

Next Row: Dc into first sc, *sc into next ch-5 sp, (dc, ch 5, dc) into next sc. Repeat from * across, ending row with sc into next ch-5 sp, (dc, ch 2, dc) into last sc. Ch 1, turn.

Next Row: Sc into first dc, *(dc, ch 5, dc) into next sc, sc into next ch-5 sp. Repeat from * across, ending row with (dc, ch 5, dc) into next sc, sc into third ch of turning-ch-5. Ch 5, turn.

For Sizes Small and Medium Only:
Next Row: Dc into first sc, *sc into next ch-5 sp, (dc, ch 5, dc) into next sc. Repeat from * across, ending row with sc into next ch-5 sp, (dc, ch 2, dc) into last sc. Ch 1, turn.

Next Row: Sc into first dc, *(dc, ch 5, dc) into next sc, sc into next ch-5 sp. Repeat from * across, ending row with (dc, ch 5, dc) into next sc, sc into third ch of turning-ch-5. Ch 5, turn.

For All Sizes:
Repeat last 7 (7, 5, 5, 5) rows 5 more times. Ch 5, turn.

Beg with Row 2 of patt, cont even in patt as established until piece measures approx 22 (21½, 21½, 21½, 21½)" from beg, ending after WS row. Ch 5, turn.

Next Row (RS): Dc into first sc, *sc into next ch-5 sp, (dc, ch 2, dc) into next ch-5 sp. Repeat from * across.

Fasten off.

FINISHING

Sew shoulder seams.

Set in sleeves. Sew sleeve and side seams.

Body Edging
With RS facing and smaller hook, attach yarn with a slip st to lower right side seam and ch 1.

Rnd 1: Work sc evenly spaced along right front lower edge, up right front opening, around back of neck, down left front opening, and along lower edge, working 2 sc at beg of each front neck shaping, 2 sc at lower front edges, and a dec sc at beg of each back neck shaping, ending rnd with a slip st to first sc. Ch 1.

Rnds 2 and 3: Same as Rnd 1.

Rnd 4: Work 1 rnd of Reverse Sc Patt around. Join with a slip st to first sc.

Fasten off.

Lower Sleeve Edging
With RS facing and smaller hook, attach yarn with a slip st to lower sleeve seam and ch 1.

Rnd 1: Work sc evenly spaced around cuff. Join with a slip st to first sc. Ch 1.

Rnd 2: Same as Rnd 1.

Rnd 3: Work 1 rnd Reverse Sc Patt around. Join with a slip st to first sc.

Fasten off.

Ilene

You'll love wearing—and making—this sweater! The unusual color palette gives it a retro look, but its fitted silhouette and flared sleeves are decidedly modern in attitude!

GAUGE

In Geometric Patt with larger hook, 16 sts and 8 rows = 4". To measure your gauge, make a test swatch as follows: Ch 18. Work Geometric Patt on 16 sts for 8 rows total. Fasten off. Piece should measure 4" square. **To save time, take time to check gauge.**

GEOMETRIC PATTERN

See chart on page 87.

NOTES

Throughout, each dc, dec dc, and turning-ch-3 counts as 1 st.

Throughout, each turning-ch-3 counts as first stitch of every row of chart. *Be sure to work the turning-ch-3 in the correct color as indicated on the chart.*

For colorwork, use intarsia technique, using separate lengths of yarn for each individual section of color.

To change color, work the last stitch of the first color until 2 loops remain on your hook, then yarn over hook with the new color and complete the stitch.

To increase, work 2 dc into 1 st.

To decrease 1 st each side, ch 3 to turn; skip first st, work a dec dc to combine next 2 sts; cont across row until 3 sts rem, ending row with dec dc to combine next 2 sts, dc into top of turning-ch-3. Ch 3, turn.

To decrease 2 sts each side, ch 3 to turn; skip first st, (work a dec dc to combine next 2 sts) twice; cont across row until 5 sts rem, ending row with (dec dc to combine next 2 sts) twice, dc into top of turning-ch-3. Ch 3, turn.

Continued on next page.

BACK

With larger hook and A, ch 71 (79, 87, 95, 103); join C (B, C, B, C) and ch 3 (counts as first dc of foundation row), cont across Row 1 of Geometric Patt. Ch 3, turn.

Cont even on 72 (80, 88, 96, 104) sts in patt as established until piece measures approx 2½ (2½, 3, 3, 3)" from beg. Ch 3, turn.

Decrease for Waist

Cont patt, dec 1 st each side every other row 5 times—62 (70, 78, 86, 94) sts rem.

Cont even in patt as established until piece measures approx 10 (10, 10½, 10½, 11)" from beg.

Increase for Bust

Cont patt, inc 1 st each side every other row 5 times—72 (80, 88, 96, 104) sts.

Cont even in patt as established until piece measures approx 16 (16¼, 16½, 16½, 17)" from beg. Fasten off.

Shape Armholes

Skip first 2 (4, 5, 6, 7) sts, and attach yarn with a slip st to next st and ch 3.

SKILL LEVEL
Advanced

SIZES
Small (Medium, Large, Extra-Large, Extra-Extra-Large). *Instructions are for smallest size, with changes for other sizes noted in parentheses as necessary.*

FINISHED MEASUREMENTS
Bust: 36 (40, 44, 48, 52)"
Total length: 23½ (24, 24½, 25, 26)"

MATERIALS
Coats and Clark's *TLC Amoré* (light worsted weight; 80% acrylic/20% nylon; each approx 6 oz/170 g and 290 yd/265 m), 3 (3, 4, 4, 5) skeins *each* of Grape #3536 (A), Red Velvet #3907 (B), Hot Pink #3752 (C), and Raspberry #3907 (D)

Crochet hooks, sizes F/5 and G/6 (3.75 and 4.00 mm) or size needed to obtain gauge

Decrease double crochet = dec dc = Yarn over hook, insert hook into next st and pull up a loop (3 loops are on your hook); yarn over hook and draw loop through 2 loops on hook (2 loops are on your hook); yarn over hook, insert hook into next st and pull up a loop (4 loops are on your hook); yarn over hook and draw loop through 2 loops on hook; yarn over hook and draw loop through all 3 loops on hook.

For sweater assembly, refer to the illustration for set-in construction on page 126.

Skip st where slip st was worked, cont patt as established until 2 (4, 5, 6, 7) sts rem in row. Ch 3, turn, leaving rest of row unworked.

Cont patt, and dec 2 sts each side every row 0 (2, 2, 5, 5) times, then dec 1 st each side every row 7 (5, 7, 4, 6) times—54 (54, 56, 56, 58) sts rem.

Cont even in patt as established until piece measures approx 23 (23½, 24, 24½, 25½)" from beg, ending after WS (RS, WS, RS, RS) row. Ch 3, turn.

Shape Neck
Skip first st, work patt as established across next 12 (12, 13, 13, 14) sts—13 (13, 14, 14, 15) sts. Fasten off.

For second side of neck, skip the middle 28 sts, and with RS (WS, RS, WS, WS) facing, attach yarn with a slip st to next st and ch 3. Skip st where slip st was worked, work patt as established to end row. Fasten off.

FRONT
Same as back until piece measures approx 16 (16½, 17, 17½, 18½)" from beg, ending after WS row. Ch 3, turn. Place marker between the middle 2 sts.

Shape Armholes and Neck
Work armhole shaping same as for back, *and at the same time,* work until 3 sts before marker, work a dec dc to combine the next 2 sts, dc into next st. Ch 3, turn, leaving rest of row unworked.

Cont armhole shaping same as for back, *and at the same time,* dec 1 st at neck edge every row 13 more times—13 (13, 14, 14, 15) sts rem.

Cont even in patt as established until piece measures approx 23½ (24, 24½, 25, 26)" from beg. Fasten off.

For second side of neck, with RS facing, attach yarn with a slip st to next st and ch 3.

Complete same as first side. Fasten off.

SLEEVES
With larger hook and A, ch 55; join C and ch 3 (counts as first dc of foundation row), cont across Row 1 of Geometric Patt—56 sts. Ch 3, turn.

Cont patt, and dec 1 st each side every other row twice, then every row 8 times—36 sts rem.

Cont even in patt as established until piece measures approx 7" from beg. Ch 3, turn.

Cont patt, and inc 1 st each side every row 1 (2, 3, 5, 9) times, then every other row 10 (10, 10, 9, 7) times—58 (60, 62, 64, 68) sts.

Cont even in patt as established until piece measures approx 18½ (19, 19½, 19½, 19½)" from beg. Fasten off.

Shape Cap
Skip first 2 (4, 5, 6, 7) sts, and attach yarn with a slip st to next st and ch 3, skip st where last slip st was worked, cont patt as established until 2 (4, 5, 6, 7) sts rem in row. Ch 3, turn, leaving rest of row unworked.

Cont patt, and dec 1 st each side every row 0 (1, 3, 5, 6) times, then dec 2 sts each side every row 8 (7, 6, 5, 5) times—22 sts rem. Fasten off.

Next Row: Skip first 3 sts, attach yarn with a slip st to next st and ch 3, skip st where last slip st was worked, cont patt as established until 3 sts rem in row. Fasten off.

Repeat last row once more—10 sts rem. Fasten off.

FINISHING

Sew shoulder seams.

Neckline Edging

With RS facing and smaller hook, attach A with a slip st to neck edge of left shoulder seam and ch 1.

Work 25 sc along left front neck edge, a dec sc at center front of neck, 25 sc along right front neck edge, and 20 sc along back neck edge—71 sts total. Join with a slip st to first sc. Fasten off.

Set in sleeves. Sew sleeve and side seams.

GEOMETRIC PATTERN

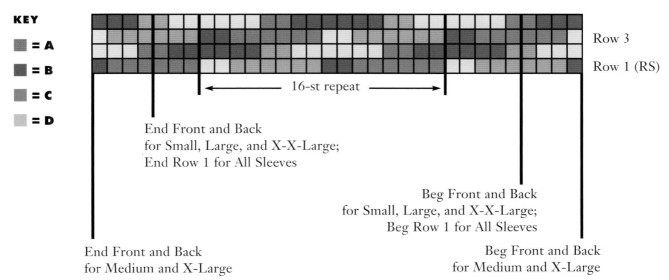

KEY

■ = A
■ = B
■ = C
■ = D

Row 3

Row 1 (RS)

16-st repeat

End Front and Back
for Small, Large, and X-X-Large;
End Row 1 for All Sleeves

Beg Front and Back
for Small, Large, and X-X-Large;
Beg Row 1 for All Sleeves

End Front and Back
for Medium and X-Large

Beg Front and Back
for Medium and X-Large

Note: Each square on chart represents one dc or turning-ch-3.

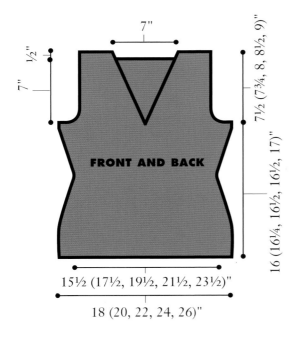

7"

½"

7"

7½ (7¾, 8, 8½, 9)"

FRONT AND BACK

16 (16¼, 16½, 16½, 17)"

15½ (17½, 19½, 21½, 23½)"

18 (20, 22, 24, 26)"

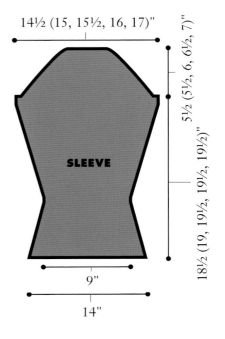

14½ (15, 15½, 16, 17)"

5½ (5½, 6, 6½, 7)"

SLEEVE

18½ (19, 19½, 19½, 19½)"

9"

14"

Nancy

Crochet this sporty pullover for yourself and you'll never want to take it off! It's made with fleecy yarn for ultimate softness.

GAUGE

In Solid Hdc Patt, with larger hook, 11 sts and 8 rows = 4". To measure your gauge, make a test swatch as follows: Ch 12. Work Solid Hdc Patt on 11 sts for 8 rows total. Fasten off. Piece should measure 4" square. **To save time, take time to check gauge.**

SOLID HALF DOUBLE CROCHET PATTERN

(any number of sts)

Foundation Row (RS): Hdc into third ch from hook and into each ch across. Ch 2, turn.

Patt Row: Skip first hdc, *hdc into next hdc. Repeat from * across, ending row with hdc into top of turning-ch-2. Ch 2, turn.

Repeat Patt Row for patt.

STRIPE PATTERN

*4 rows A, 4 rows B. Repeat from * for patt.

SIDEWAYS RIB PATTERN

(any number of sts)

Foundation Row (RS): Sc into second ch from hook and into each ch across. Ch 1, turn.

Patt Row: Sc *through the back loop only* of each sc across. Ch 1, turn.

Repeat Patt Row.

NOTES

Throughout, each hdc, dec hdc, and turning-ch-2 counts as 1 st.

Continued on next page.

BACK

With larger hook, ch 41 (47, 55, 61, 69, 77).

Foundation Row (RS): Hdc into third ch from hook and into each ch across— 40 (46, 54, 60, 68, 76) sts. Ch 2, turn.

Cont in Solid Hdc Patt in Stripe Patt, and inc 1 st each side every sixth row once, then every fourth row 4 times— 50 (56, 64, 70, 78, 86) sts.

Cont even in patts as established until piece measures approx 13½ (13½, 14, 14, 14, 14)" from beg. *Do not ch 2.* Turn.

Shape Armholes

Next Row: Slip st into first 4 (5, 7, 8, 10, 13) sts, ch 2, skip st where last slip st was worked, cont patts as established until 3 (4, 6, 7, 9, 12) sts rem in row. Ch 2, turn, leaving rest of row unworked—44 (48, 52, 56, 60, 62) sts rem.

Cont patts as established, and dec 1 st each side every row 3 (4, 7, 8, 11, 11) times, then dec 1 st each side every other row 2 (2, 1, 1, 0, 0) times— 34 (36, 36, 38, 38, 40) sts rem.

SKILL LEVEL

Advanced Beginner

SIZES

Small (Medium, Large, Extra-Large, Extra-Extra-Large, Extra-Extra-Extra-Large). *Instructions are for smallest size, with changes for other sizes noted in parentheses as necessary.*

FINISHED MEASUREMENTS

Bust: 36 (39½, 43, 47, 51, 54½)"
Total length: 21 (21¼, 22, 22½, 23, 23)"

MATERIALS

Muench/GGH's *Esprit* (bulky weight; 100% nylon; each approx 1¾ oz/50 g and 88 yd/80 m), 6 (7, 7, 8, 8, 9) balls Kiwi #22 (A) and 5 (6, 6, 7, 7, 8) balls Apple #15 (B)

Crochet hooks, sizes J/10 and K/10.5 (6.00 and 6.50 mm) or size needed to obtain gauge

To increase 1 st each side, ch 2 to turn; skip first st, work 2 hdc into next st; cont patt as established until 2 sts rem, ending row with 2 hdc into next st, hdc into top of turning-ch-2. Ch 2, turn.

To decrease 1 st each side, ch 2 to turn; skip first st, work a dec hdc to combine next 2 sts; cont patt as established until 3 sts rem, ending row with dec hdc to combine next 2 sts, hdc into top of turning-ch-2. Ch 2, turn.

To decrease 2 sts each side, ch 2 to turn; skip first st, (work a dec hdc to combine next 2 sts) twice; cont patt as established until 5 sts rem, ending row with (dec hdc to combine next 2 sts) twice, hdc into top of turning-ch-2. Ch 2, turn.

Decrease half double crochet = dec hdc = Yarn over hook, insert hook into next st and pull up a loop (3 loops are on your hook); yarn over hook, insert hook into next st and pull up a loop; yarn over hook and draw loop through all 5 loops on hook.

For sweater assembly, refer to the illustration for set-in construction on page 126.

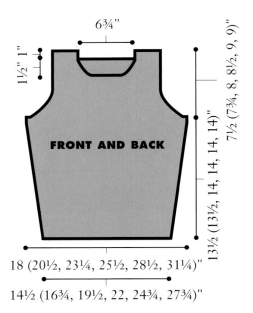

6¾"

1½" 1"

FRONT AND BACK

7½ (7¾, 8, 8½, 9, 9)"

13½ (13½, 14, 14, 14, 14)"

18 (20½, 23¼, 25½, 28½, 31¼)"

14½ (16¾, 19½, 22, 24¾, 27¾)"

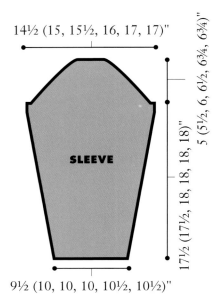

14½ (15, 15½, 16, 17, 17)"

5 (5½, 6, 6½, 6¾, 6¾)"

SLEEVE

17½ (17½, 18, 18, 18, 18)"

9½ (10, 10, 10, 10½, 10½)"

Cont even, if necessary, in patts as established until piece measures approx 20 (20¼, 21, 21½, 22, 22)" from beg, ending after WS row. Ch 2, turn.

Shape Neck
Work patts as established across first 9 (10, 10, 11, 11, 12) sts. Ch 2, turn, leaving rest of row unworked.

Cont patts as established, and dec 1 st at neck edge once—8 (9, 9, 10, 10, 11) sts rem. Ch 2, turn.

Cont even, if necessary, in patts as established until this side measures approx 21 (21¼, 22, 22½, 23, 23)" from beg.

Fasten off.

For second side of neck, with RS facing, maintaining Stripe Patt as established, skip the middle 16 sts and attach yarn with a slip st to next st and ch 2.

Complete same as first side.

FRONT
Same as back until piece measures approx 18½ (18¾, 19½, 20, 20½, 20½)" from beg, ending after WS row. Ch 2, turn.

Shape Neck
Next Row (RS): Work patts as established across first 12 (13, 13, 14, 14, 15) sts. Ch 2, turn, leaving rest of row unworked.

Cont patts as established, and dec 1 st at neck edge every row 4 times—8 (9, 9, 10, 10, 11) sts rem. Ch 2, turn.

Cont even, if necessary, in patts as established until this side measures same as back.

Fasten off.

For second side of neck, with RS facing, maintaining Stripe Patt as established, skip the middle 10 sts, and attach yarn with a slip st to next st and ch 2.

Complete same as first side.

SLEEVES

With larger hook, ch 27 (28, 28, 29, 30, 30).

Foundation Row (RS): Hdc into third ch from hook and into each ch across 26 (27, 27, 28, 29, 29) sts. Ch 2, turn.

Cont in Solid Hdc Patt in Stripe Patt, and inc 1 st each side every other row 0 (0, 0, 0, 1, 1) times, every fourth row 4 (4, 7, 7, 8, 8) times, then every sixth row 3 (3, 1, 1, 0, 0) times—40 (41, 43, 44, 47, 47) sts.

Cont even, if necessary, in patts as established until piece measures approx 17½ (17½, 18, 18, 18, 18)" from beg. *Do not ch 2.* Turn.

Shape Cap

Next Row (RS): Slip st into first 4 (5, 7, 8, 10, 13) sts, ch 2, skip st where last slip st was worked, cont patts as established until 3 (4, 6, 7, 9, 12) sts rem in row. Ch 2, turn, leaving rest of row unworked—34 (33, 31, 30, 29, 23) sts rem.

Cont patts as established, and dec 1 st each side every fourth row 0 (0, 0, 0, 0, 2) times, every other row 0 (0, 2, 3, 4, 1) times, every row 5 (7, 4, 3, 2, 0) times, then dec 2 sts each side every row 1 (0, 0, 0, 0, 0) times—20 (19, 19, 18, 17, 17) sts rem. Ch 2, turn.

Next Row: Work even in patts as established. *Do not ch 2.* Turn.

Next Row: Slip st into first 3 sts, ch 2. Skip st where last slip st was worked, hdc into each st across until 2 sts rem—16 (15, 15, 14, 13, 13) sts.

Next Row: Slip st into first 3 sts, ch 2. Skip st where last slip st was worked, hdc into each st across until 2 sts rem—12 (11, 11, 10, 9, 9) sts.

Fasten off.

FINISHING

Sew shoulder seams.

With RS facing and smaller hook, attach A with a slip st to neck edge of left shoulder seam and ch 1.

Work 40 sc evenly spaced around neckline. Join with a slip st to first sc.

Fasten off.

Neckband

With smaller hook and A, ch 13.

Work even in Sideways Rib Patt on 12 sts until neckband, when slightly stretched, fits around neckline. Fasten off.

Sew foundation row of neckband to the last row of the neckband. Sew neckband into place onto neckline, placing seam at center of back neck.

Set in sleeves. Sew side and sleeve seams.

Cassie

This useful bag is sturdy enough to tote around all of your daily essentials. Its secret? A lightweight sheet of plastic canvas sandwiched between the crocheted fabric and lining.

GAUGE

In patt, 16 sts and 10 rows = 4". To measure your gauge, make a test swatch as follows: Ch 17.

Foundation Row (RS): Hdc into third ch from hook and into each ch across—15 hdc plus the turning-ch-2. Ch 2, turn.

Next Row: Skip first hdc, hdc into each hdc across, ending row with hdc into top of turning-ch-2—15 hdc plus the turning-ch-2. Ch 2, turn.

Repeat last row 8 more times.

Fasten off.

Piece should measure 4" square. **To save time, take time to check gauge.**

STRIPE PATTERN

*4 rnds B, 1 rnd A, 4 rnds C, 1 rnd A. Repeat from * for patt.

NOTES

Throughout, each sc, hdc, and ch-2 counts as 1 st; each ch-1 *does not* count as 1 st.

When making bottom and body of bag, RS always faces you.

Constructionwise, this tote bag is made in the round.

BOTTOM

With A, ch 23.

Rnd 1 (RS): Sc into second ch from hook and into next 20 ch, 5 sc into last ch; *working into unused loops of foundation ch,* sc into next 20 ch, 4 sc into last ch—50 sts. Join with a slip st to first sc. Ch 1.

Rnd 2: Sc into same sc as slip st, sc into next 21 sc, (2 sc into next sc) 3 times, sc into next 22 sc, (2 sc into next sc) 3 times—56 sts. Join with a slip st to first sc. Ch 1.

Rnd 3: Sc into same sc as slip st, sc into next 22 sc, (2 sc into next sc, sc into next sc) twice, 2 sc into next sc, sc into next 23 sc, (2 sc into next sc, sc into next sc) twice, 2 sc into next sc—62 sts. Join with a slip st to first sc. Ch 1.

Rnd 4: Sc into same sc as slip st, sc into next 21 sc, (2 sc into next sc, sc into next 2 sc) twice, 2 sc into next sc, sc into next 24 sc, (2 sc into next sc, sc into next 2 sc) twice, 2 sc into next sc, sc into next 2 sc—68 sts. Join with a slip st to first sc. Ch 1.

SKILL LEVEL
Advanced Beginner

FINISHED MEASUREMENTS
Approx 10" long and 10" wide and 4½" high

MATERIALS
Tahki-Stacy Charles's *Willow* (heavy worsted weight; 66% linen/34% cotton; each approx 1¾ oz/50 g and 81 yd/75 m), 2 balls *each* of Coffee #014 (A), Sun #013 (B), and Persimmon #005 (C)

Crochet hook, size H/8 (5.00 mm) or size needed to obtain gauge

Three sheets of plastic canvas, 10½" wide and 13½" long

Matching fabric for lining, approx ½ yd

Rnd 5: Sc into same sc as slip st, sc into next 24 sc, (2 sc into next sc, sc into next 3 sc) twice, 2 sc into next sc, sc into next 25 sc, (2 sc into next sc, sc into next 3 sc) twice, 2 sc into next sc—74 sts. Join with a slip st to first sc. Ch 1.

Rnd 6: Sc into same sc as slip st, sc into next 23 sc, (2 sc into next sc, sc into next 4 sc) twice, 2 sc into next sc, sc into next 26 sc, (2 sc into next sc, sc into next 4 sc) twice, 2 sc into next sc, sc into next 2 sc—80 sts. Join with a slip st to first sc. Ch 1.

Rnd 7: Sc into same sc as slip st, sc into next 22 sc, (2 sc into next sc, sc into next 5 sc) twice, 2 sc into next sc, sc into next 27 sc, (2 sc into next sc, sc into next 5 sc) twice, 2 sc into next sc, sc into next 4 sc—86 sts. Join with a slip st to first sc. Ch 1.

Rnd 8: Sc into same sc as slip st, sc into next 21 sc, (2 sc into next sc, sc into next 6 sc) twice, 2 sc into next sc, sc into next 28 sc, (2 sc into next sc, sc into next 6 sc) 3 times—92 sts. Join with a slip st to first sc. Ch 1.

Rnd 9: Sc into same sc as slip st, sc into next 28 sc, (2 sc into next sc, sc into next 7 sc) twice, 2 sc into next sc, sc into next 29 sc, (2 sc into next sc, sc into next 7 sc) twice, 2 sc into next sc—98 sts. Change to B. Join with a slip st to first sc.

BODY

Rnd 1 (RS): *Working into back loops only,* cont with B, ch 2, skip first sc, hdc into next sc and into each sc around, ending rnd with a slip st to top of ch-2—98 sts.

Rnd 2: Ch 2, skip st where slip st was worked, hdc into next hdc and into each hdc around, ending rnd with a slip st to top of ch-2—98 sts.

Rnds 3-25: As Rnd 2, working in Stripe Patt—98 sts each rnd.

Rnd 26: Ch 1, *then working left to right,* sc into next hdc and into each hdc around, ending rnd with a slip st to first sc—98 sts.

Fasten off.

FINISHING

Bottom Trim

With RS facing, attach A with a slip st to unused loop of any st from Rnd 9 of bottom of bag and ch 1.

Working into free loops from Rnd 9 of bottom of bag, work 98 slip sts around. Join with a slip st to first slip st.

Fasten off.

Using bottom as a guide, cut 1 piece of plastic canvas to fit.

Cut 2 pieces of plastic canvas to height of bag less ½"; overlap short edges by ½" and sew into a tube. Sew tube to bottom piece of plastic canvas.

Place plastic canvas into bag and whipstitch ½" down from upper edge of bag on WS.

Handles *(Make 4)*

With C, ch 108.

Row 1 (RS): Sc into second ch from hook and into each ch across—107 sts. Ch 1, turn.

Row 2: Sc into each sc across—107 sts.

Fasten off.

With WS tog, crochet 2 handles tog to form a double-thick handle as follows: Attach A with a slip st through both thicknesses at beg of last row worked, and ch 1.

Work 1 rnd of sc evenly spaced around, working through both thicknesses of handles, working 3 sc into each corner. Join with a slip st to first sc.

Fasten off.

Sew a strap onto each side of bag and plastic canvas as shown in the photograph to the right, overlapping 2" on RS.

Using bottom of bag as a guide, cut lining to fit, adding ½" all around.

Cut lining to fit inside of bag. Sew lining to bottom piece of lining. Place lining inside bag, turn under top edge, and whipstitch to top of bag, covering plastic canvas.

Natalie

Perfect for summertime stitching, this little halter sports an unexpected touch—sparkly glass beads are added to each picot in the lower edging. It's fun yet very easy to make!

GAUGE

In Textured Patt with larger hook, 22 sts and 16 rows = 4". To measure your gauge, make a test swatch as follows: With larger hook, ch 23. Work Textured Patt on 22 sts for 16 rows total. Fasten off. Piece should measure 4" square. **To save time, take time to check gauge.**

TEXTURED PATTERN

(mult 2 + 1 sts)

Foundation Row (RS): Sc into third ch from hook, *dc into next ch, sc into next ch. Repeat from * across, ending row with hdc into last ch. Ch 2, turn.

Patt Row: Skip first hdc, *sc into next sc, dc into next dc. Repeat from * across, ending row with sc into next sc, hdc into top of turning-ch-2. Ch 2, turn.

Repeat Patt Row for patt.

NOTES

Throughout, each sc, hdc, dc, dec hdc, and turning-ch-2 counts as 1 st.

Bead ch = Move a bead up next to the hook, yarn over hook and draw loop through the loop on the hook, locking bead into the st.

Decrease half double crochet = dec hdc = Yarn over hook, insert hook into next st and pull up a loop (3 loops are on your hook); yarn over hook, insert hook into next st and pull up a loop; yarn over hook and draw loop through all 5 loops on hook.

HALTER

With larger hook, ch 104.

Work Foundation Row of Textured Patt—103 sts. Ch 2, turn.

Next Row (WS): Skip first hdc, work a dec hdc to combine next 2 sts, *sc into next sc, dc into next dc. Repeat from * across until 4 sts rem, ending row with sc into next sc, dec hdc to combine next 2 sts, hdc into top of turning-ch-2. Ch 2, turn.

Next Row: Skip first hdc, work a dec hdc to combine next 2 sts, *dc into next dc, sc into next sc. Repeat from * across until 4 sts rem, ending row with dc into next dc, dec hdc to combine next 2 sts, hdc into top of turning-ch-2. Ch 2, turn.

Repeat last 2 rows 18 more times— 27 sts rem. Ch 2, turn.

Cont even in patt as established for 3 rows.

Fasten off.

SKILL LEVEL
Advanced Beginner

SIZES
One size fits all

MATERIALS
Aurora Yarn/Ornaghi Filati's *Safran* (sport weight; 100% Egyptian cotton; each approx 1¾ oz/50 g and 175 yd/160 m), 3 balls Cherry Red #19

Crochet hooks, sizes D/3 and E/4 (3.25 and 3.50 mm) or size needed to obtain gauge

Seventeen glass beads, 6 mm

COOL TIP For a longer garment, crochet evenly in Textured Pattern on 103 stitches for several rows before beginning the decreases.

Left Tie and Side Edging

With smaller hook, ch 121. Slip st into second ch from hook and into next 119 ch; with RS facing, attach tie with a slip st to beg of Row 1 of lower edging, and ch 1. Work 50 sc evenly spaced along side of halter.

Fasten off.

Right Tie and Side Edging

With RS facing and smaller hook, attach yarn with a slip st to other neck edge of halter, and ch 1. Work 50 sc evenly spaced along side of halter, ending at Row 1 of lower edging; ch 121, slip st into second ch from hook and into next 119 ch. Join with a slip st to last sc.

Fasten off.

Upper Tie

With smaller hook, ch 161. Slip st into second ch from hook and into next 159 ch.

Fasten off.

Fold last 3 rows of halter to WS and whipstitch into place to form a casing.

Thread upper tie through casing.

FINISHING

Lower Edging

Prethread all 17 beads onto yarn.

With RS facing and smaller hook, attach yarn with the beads prethreaded to the lower right edge of halter with a slip st, and ch 1.

Row 1 (RS): Working into unused loops of foundation chain, work 103 sc along lower edge. Ch 3, turn.

Row 2: Skip first 3 sc, *(2 dc, ch 3, 2 dc) into next sc, skip next 2 sc, dc into next sc, skip next 2 sc. Repeat from * across, ending row with (2 dc, ch 3, 2 dc) into next sc, skip next 2 sc, dc into last sc. Ch 3, turn.

Rows 3 and 4: Skip first 3 dc, *(2 dc, ch 3, 2 dc) into next ch-3 sp, skip next 2 dc, dc into next dc, skip next 2 dc. Repeat from * across, ending row with (2 dc, ch 3, 2 dc) into next ch-3 sp, skip next 2 dc, dc into top of turning-ch-3. Ch 3, turn.

Row 5: Skip first 3 dc, *(2 dc, ch 1, bead ch, ch 1, 2 dc) into next ch-3 sp, skip next 2 dc, dc into next dc, skip next 2 dc. Repeat from * across, ending row with (2 dc, ch 1, bead ch, ch 1, 2 dc) into next ch-3 sp, skip next 2 dc, dc into top of turning-ch-3.

Fasten off.

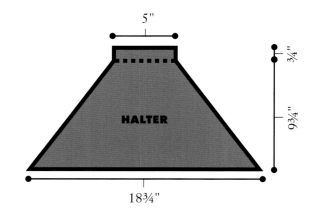

Note: Measurements in schematic drawing do not include edging.

Andrea

This colorful drawstring bag has an unusual construction: It's composed of textured triangular motifs sewn together. Whip up a few pieces in a sitting, and before you know it you'll have enough to complete this bag.

GAUGE

In patt, each Triangle Motif measures 2½" along each side. To measure your gauge, make a test swatch as follows: Ch 6. Work Rows 1–6 of Triangle Motif. Fasten off. Piece should measure 2½" along each side. **To save time, take time to check gauge.**

TRIANGLE MOTIF A

With A, ch 6.

Row 1 (WS): Sc into second ch from hook, sc into next 4 ch; ch 2; working into unused loops of foundation chain, sc into next 5 ch. Ch 2, turn.

Row 2: Working into back loop only, sc into second ch from hook, sc into next 5 sc, sc into next ch; ch 2; along other side, *working into back loop only,* sc into next ch and into next 5 sc. Change to B, ch 2, turn.

Row 3: Working into back look only, sc into second ch from hook, sc into next 6 sc, sc into next ch; ch 2; along other side, *working into back loop only,* sc into next ch and into next 7 sc. Ch 2, turn.

Row 4: Working into back look only, sc into second ch from hook, sc into next 8 sc, sc into next ch; ch 2; along other side, *working into back loop only,* sc into next ch and into next 8 sc. Fasten off B. Change to A, ch 2, turn.

Row 5: Working into back look only, sc into second ch from hook, sc into next 9 sc, sc into next ch; ch 2; along other side, *working into back loop only,* sc into next ch and into next 10 sc. Ch 2, turn.

Continued on next page.

BOTTOM

With A, ch 2.

Rnd 1 (RS): 7 sc into second ch from hook. Join with a slip st to first sc. Ch 1.

Rnd 2: 2 sc into each sc around—14 sc. Join with a slip st to first sc. Ch 1.

Rnd 3: *Sc into next sc, 2 sc into next sc. Repeat from * around—21 sc. Join with a slip st to first sc. Ch 1.

Rnd 4: *Sc into next 2 sc, 2 sc into next sc. Repeat from * around—28 sc. Join with a slip st to first sc. Ch 1.

Rnd 5: *Sc into next 3 sc, 2 sc into next sc. Repeat from * around—35 sc. Join with a slip st to first sc. Ch 1.

Rnd 6: *Sc into next 4 sc, 2 sc into next sc. Repeat from * around—42 sc. Join with a slip st to first sc. Ch 1.

Rnd 7: *Sc into next 5 sc, 2 sc into next sc. Repeat from * around—49 sc. Join with a slip st to first sc. Ch 1.

Rnd 8: *Sc into next 6 sc, 2 sc into next sc. Repeat from * around—56 sc. Join with a slip st to first sc. Ch 1.

Rnd 9: *Sc into next 7 sc, 2 sc into next sc. Repeat from * around—63 sc. Join with a slip st to first sc. Ch 1.

SKILL LEVEL
Intermediate

FINISHED MEASUREMENTS
Approx 5¾" wide and 12½" long

MATERIALS
Plymouth's *Wildflower* (light worsted weight; 51% cotton/ 49% acrylic; each approx 1¾ oz/50 g and 136 yd/ 124 m), 3 balls Turquoise #55 (A) and 2 balls Lime #58 (B)

Crochet hook, size E/4 (3.50 mm) or size needed to obtain gauge

Four beads with large holes

Row 6: *Working into back loop only,* sc into second ch from hook, sc into next 11 sc, sc into next ch; ch 2; along other side, *working into back loop only,* sc into next ch and into next 11 sc.

Fasten off.

TRIANGLE MOTIF B

Same as Triangle Motif A *except* beg with B and reverse colors.

NOTES

When making bottom of bag, RS always faces you.

When making motifs, always work *into the back loop only* of each ch or sc.

To change color, work last stitch of the first color until 2 loops remain on your hook, then yarn over hook with the new color and complete the stitch.

Rnd 10: *Sc into next 8 sc, 2 sc into next sc. Repeat from * around—70 sc. Join with a slip st to first sc. Ch 1.

Rnd 11: *Sc into next 9 sc, 2 sc into next sc. Repeat from * around—77 sc. Join with a slip st to first sc. Ch 1.

Rnd 12: *Sc into next 10 sc, 2 sc into next sc. Repeat from * around—84 sc. Join with a slip st to first sc.

Fasten off.

BODY

Make 21 pieces *each* of Triangle Motif A and Triangle Motif B.

With RS facing, make 3 rings of 14 motifs each, whipstitching tog *through back loops only* and alternating Triangle Motif A and Triangle Motif B as seen in the photograph on facing page.

Whipstitch rings tog.

FINISHING

Ruffled Top

With RS facing, attach A with a slip st to any ch-2 sp at top of bag.

Rnd 1 (RS): Work 84 sc evenly spaced around top of bag. Join with a slip st to first sc.

Rnd 2: Ch 3, skip st where last slip st was worked, work 83 dc around. Join with a slip st to top of ch-3. Ch 3.

COOL TIP Make your bag a kaleido-scope of color! Crochet the motifs using bits of scrap yarn—just be sure to choose yarns with similar weight and laundering instructions.

Rnds 3-6: As Rnd 2. At the end of Rnd 6, ch 4 instead of ch 3.

Rnd 7: Skip st where last slip st was worked, *dc into next dc, ch 1, skip next dc. Repeat from * around, ending rnd with a slip st to third ch of ch-4. Ch 3.

Rnd 8: Skip st where last slip st was worked, *dc into ch-1 sp, dc into next dc. Repeat from * around, ending rnd with a slip st to top of ch-3. Ch 3.

Rnds 9-11: Skip st where last slip st was worked, dc into each dc around. Join with a slip st to top of ch-3. Ch 1.

Rnd 12: Sc into first dc, *ch 3, slip st into third ch from hook, skip next dc, sc into next sc. Repeat from * around, ending rnd with ch 3, slip st into third ch from hook, skip next dc, slip st to first sc.

Fasten off.

Ties *(Make 2)*

With B, ch 135. Slip st into each ch across.

Fasten off.

Thread each tie through the ch-1 spaces of Rnd 7, starting the second tie halfway around.

Place a bead on each end of each tie, securing with an overhand knot. Knot ties tog.

Holly

Casual and comfortable, this striped tunic will complement lots of things in your wardrobe. Make one as a cover-up for your favorite swimsuit!

GAUGE

In Cluster Patt, 23 sts and 14 rows = 4". To measure your gauge, make a test swatch as follows: Ch 28. Work Cluster Patt on 27 sts for 16 rows total. Fasten off. Piece should measure 4½" square. **To save time, take time to check gauge.**

CLUSTER PATTERN

(mult 5 + 2 sts)

Foundation Row (WS): Sc into second ch from hook and into each ch across. Ch 3, turn.

Row 1 (RS): Skip first 3 sc, *5 dc into next sc, skip next 4 sc. Repeat from * across, ending row with 5 dc into next sc, skip next 2 sc, dc into last sc. Ch 5, turn.

Row 2: Skip first dc, *5-dc cluster to combine the next 5 dc, ch 4. Repeat from * across, ending row with 5-dc cluster to combine the next 5 dc, ch 2, dc into third ch of turning-ch-3. Ch 1, turn.

Row 3: Sc into first dc, 2 sc into ch-2 sp, *sc into top of 5-dc cluster, 4 sc into next ch-4 sp. Repeat from * across, ending row with sc into top of 5-dc cluster, 2 sc under turning-ch-5, sc into third ch of turning-ch-5. Change color, ch 1, turn.

Row 4: Sc into each sc across. Ch 3, turn.

Repeat Rows 1-4 for patt.

STRIPE PATTERN

*4 rows A, 4 rows B, 4 rows C. Repeat from * for patt.

Continued on next page.

BACK

With A, ch 108 (118, 128, 138, 148, 158).

Beg Cluster Patt, and work even on 107 (117, 127, 137, 147, 157) sts in Stripe Patt until piece measures approx 21" from beg, ending after Row 3 of patt.

Fasten off.

Shape Armholes

Skip first 15 (20, 20, 25, 25, 30) sts, and with WS facing, attach next color with a slip st to next st and ch 1. Sc into same st as slip st and into next 76 (76, 86, 86, 96, 96) sts. Ch 3, turn, leaving rest of row unworked.

Cont even on 77 (77, 87, 87, 97, 97) sts in patts as established until piece measures approx 27½ (27½, 28½, 28½, 28½, 28½)" from beg, ending after Row 3 of patt. Change color, ch 1, turn.

Shape Neck

Next Row (WS): Sc into first 24 (24, 29, 29, 34, 34) sc. Ch 3, turn, leaving rest of row unworked.

Next Row: Skip first 3 sc, (5 dc into next sc, skip next 4 sc) 3 (3, 4, 4, 5, 5) times, 5 dc into next sc, skip next 2 sc, dc into next sc. Ch 5, turn.

SKILL LEVEL
Intermediate

SIZES
Small (Medium, Large, Extra-Large, Extra-Extra-Large, Extra-Extra-Extra Large). *Instructions are for smallest size, with changes for other sizes noted in parentheses as necessary.*

FINISHED MEASUREMENTS
Bust: 37 (41, 44, 48, 51, 55)"
Total length: 29 (29, 30, 30, 30, 30)"

MATERIALS
Paton's *Grace* (sport weight; 100% cotton; each approx 1¾ oz/50 g and 136 yd/125 m), 7 (8, 9, 9, 10, 10) balls Terracotta #60604 (A), 6 (7, 8, 9, 9, 10) balls Apricot #60603 (B), and 7 (8, 9, 9, 10, 10) balls Ginger #60027 (C)

Crochet hook, size E/4 (3.50 mm) or size needed to obtain gauge

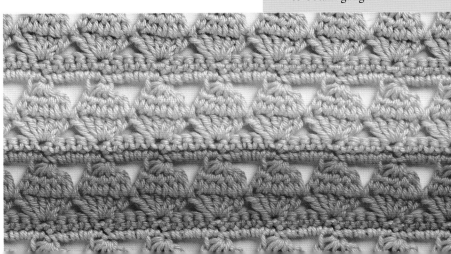

Throughout, each sc, dc, and 5-dc cluster counts as 1 st; each ch-4 sp counts as 4 sts; each ch-2 sp counts as 2 sts; each turning-ch-5 counts as 3 sts.

5-dc cluster = (Yarn over, insert hook into next st and pull up a loop, yarn over hook and draw loop through 2 loops on hook) 5 times, yarn over hook and draw loop through all 6 loops on hook.

Decrease single crochet = dec sc = (Insert hook into next st and draw up a loop) twice, yarn over hook and draw loop through all 3 loops on hook.

For sweater assembly, refer to the illustration for square indented construction on page 126.

Cont even on 22 (22, 27, 27, 32, 32) sts in patts as established until this side measures approx 29 (29, 30, 30, 30, 30)" from beg.

Fasten off.

For second side of neck, maintaining Stripe Patt as established, skip the middle 29 sts, and with WS facing, attach yarn with a slip st to next st and ch 1.

Complete same as first side.

FRONT

Same as back until piece measures approx 24½ (24½, 25½, 25½, 25½, 25½)" from beg, ending after Row 3 of patt. Change color, ch 1, turn.

Shape Neck

Next Row (WS): Sc into first 24 (24, 29, 29, 34, 34) sc. Ch 3, turn, leaving rest of row unworked.

Next Row: Skip first 3 sc, (5 dc into next sc, skip next 4 sc) 3 (3, 4, 4, 5, 5) times, 5 dc into next sc, skip next 2 sc, dc into next sc. Ch 5, turn.

Cont even on 22 (22, 27, 27, 32, 32) sts in patts as established until this side measures approx 29 (29, 30, 30, 30, 30)" from beg.

Fasten off.

For second side of neck, maintaining Stripe Patt as established, skip the middle 29 sts, and with WS facing, attach yarn with a slip st to next st and ch 1.

Complete same as first side.

SLEEVES

With A, ch 63 (63, 68, 68, 73, 78).

Work even in Cluster Patt on 62 (62, 67, 67, 72, 77) sts in Stripe Patt until piece measures approx 1" from beg, ending after Row 3 of patt. Change color. Ch 1, turn.

Increase Row 1 (WS): 2 sc into first sc, sc into each sc across until 1 sc rem, ending row with 2 sc into last sc. Ch 3, turn.

Increase Row 2: Dc into first sc, dc into next sc, skip next 2 sc, *5 dc into next sc, skip next 4 sc. Repeat from * across, ending row with 5 dc into next sc, skip next 2 sc, dc into next sc, 2 dc into last sc. Ch 3, turn.

Increase Row 3: Dc into first dc, dc into next 2 dc, ch 2, *5-dc cluster to combine next 5 dc, ch 4. Repeat from * across, ending row with 5-dc cluster to combine next 5 dc, ch 2, dc into next 2 dc, 2 dc into top of turning-ch-3. Ch 1, turn.

Increase Row 4: 2 sc into first dc, sc into next 3 dc, 2 sc into ch-2 sp, *sc into top of next 5-dc cluster, 4 sc into next ch-4 sp. Repeat from * across, ending row with sc into top of next 5-dc cluster, 2 sc into ch-2 sp, sc into next 3 dc, 2 sc into top of turning-ch-3. Change color. Ch 1, turn.

Increase Row 5: Same as Sleeve Increase Row 1. Ch 5, turn.

Increase Row 6: Skip first 3 sc, *5 dc into next sc, skip next 4 sc. Repeat from * across, ending row with 5 dc into next sc, ch 2, skip next 2 sc, dc into last sc. Ch 5, turn.

***Increase Row* 7:** Skip first dc and ch-2 sp, *5-dc cluster to combine next 5 dc, ch 4. Repeat from * across, ending row with 5-dc cluster to combine next 5 dc, ch 2, dc into third ch of turning-ch-5. Ch 1, turn.

***Increase Row* 8:** Sc into first dc, 2 sc into next ch-2 sp, *sc into top of 5-dc cluster, 4 sc into next ch-4 sp. Repeat from * across, ending row with sc into top of 5-dc cluster, 2 sc under turning-ch-5, sc into third ch of turning-ch-5. Change color. Ch 1, turn.

Cont even in patts as established for 16 (16, 16, 12, 12, 12) rows.

Repeat Sleeve Increase Rows 1-8 once more.

Cont even in patts as established for 20 (20, 16, 16, 12, 12) rows.

Repeat Sleeve Increase Rows 1-8 once more—92 (92, 97, 97, 102, 107) sts. Change color. Ch 1, turn.

Cont even in patts as established until piece measures approx 22 (22, 21½, 21½, 21, 21)" from beg.

Fasten off.

FINISHING

Sew shoulder seams.

Neckline Edging

With RS facing, attach A with a slip st to neck edge of left shoulder seam and ch 1.

Work 141 sc evenly spaced around neckline, working a dec sc at beg of each side of front and back neck shaping. Join with a slip st to first sc.

Fasten off.

Set in sleeves.

Sew sleeve and side seams, leaving lower 5" open for side slits.

Lower Edging

With RS facing, attach A with a slip st to lower edge of right side seam and ch 1.

Work 31 sc down front of right side slit, 3 sc at lower right front corner, 107 (117, 127, 137, 147, 157) sc along lower edge of front, 3 sc at lower left front corner, 31 sc up left side slit, dec sc at top of side slit, 31 sc down left side slit, 3 sc at lower back corner, 107 (117, 127, 137, 147, 157) sc along lower edge of back, 3 sc at lower right back corner, 31 sc up right side slit, dec sc at top of side slit—352 (372, 392, 412, 432, 452) sts total. Join with a slip st to first sc.

Fasten off.

Sleeve Edging

With RS facing, attach A with a slip st to lower sleeve seam and ch 1.

Working into unused loops of foundation chain, work 62 (62, 67, 67, 72, 77) sc around lower edge of sleeve. Join with a slip st to first sc.

Fasten off.

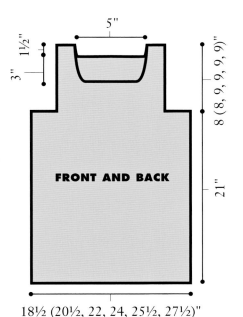

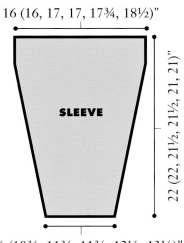

Note: Measurements in schematic drawings do not include lower edging.

Patti

Think all crocheted fabrics look alike? Here's a new take on a knitted favorite: a traditional panel of honeycomb and popcorn stitches!

GAUGE

In Solid Hdc Patt, with larger hook, 17 sts and 12 rows = 4". To measure your gauge, make a test swatch as follows: Ch 18. Work Solid Hdc Patt on 17 sts for 12 rows total. Fasten off. Piece should measure 4" square. **To save time, take time to check gauge.**

SOLID HALF DOUBLE CROCHET PATTERN

(any number of sts)

Foundation Row (RS): Hdc into third ch from hook and into each ch across. Ch 2, turn.

Patt Row: Skip first hdc, *hdc into next hdc. Repeat from * across, ending row with hdc into top of turning-ch-2. Ch 2, turn.

Repeat Patt Row for patt.

ARAN PANEL PATTERN

(over the middle 28 sts)

Row 1 (RS): Rope St, skip the hdc behind the Rope St just made, hdc into the next 3 hdc, Rope St, skip the hdc behind the Rope St just made, hdc into the next hdc, skip the next 2 sts, FPDTR into the next 2 sts two rows below, skip the 2 sts behind the 2 FPDTR just made, hdc into the next 4 sts, FPDTR into the 2 sts two rows below that are immediately to the left of the last 2 FPDTR made, skip the next 4 sts two rows below, FPDTR into the next 2 sts two rows below, skip the next 4 sts, hdc into the next 4 sts, FPDTR into the 2 sts two rows below that are immediately to the left of the last 2 FPDTR made, skip the next 2 sts, hdc into the next hdc, Rope St, skip the hdc behind the Rope St just made, hdc into the next 3 hdc, Rope St, skip the hdc behind the Rope St just made.

Continued on next page.

BACK

With larger hook, ch 75 (83, 91, 99, 107, 115).

Foundation Row 1 (RS): Hdc into third ch from hook and into each ch across—74 (82, 90, 98, 106, 114) sts. Ch 2, turn.

Foundation Row 2: Skip first st, hdc into each hdc across, ending row with hdc into top of turning-ch-2—74 (82, 90, 98, 106, 114) sts. Ch 2, turn.

Set Up Patts

Next Row (RS): Skip the first st, hdc into the next 22 (26, 30, 34, 38, 42) sts, work Row 1 of Aran Panel Patt over the middle 28 sts, hdc into the next 22 (26, 30, 34, 38, 42) sts, hdc into top of turning-ch-2. Ch 2, turn.

Cont even in Solid Hdc Patt with Aran Panel Patt over the middle 28 sts as established until piece measures approx 12½" from beg, ending after WS row. *Do not ch 2.* Turn.

SKILL LEVEL
Advanced

SIZES
Extra-Small (Small, Medium, Large, Extra-Large, Extra-Extra-Large). *Instructions are for smallest size, with changes for other sizes noted in parentheses as necessary.*

FINISHED MEASUREMENTS
Bust: 36 (39½, 43, 47, 51, 54½)"
Total length: 20 (20¼, 20½, 21, 21½, 21½)"

MATERIALS
Lion Brand's *Wool-Ease* (worsted weight; 80% acrylic/20% wool; each approx 3 oz/85 g and 197 yd/180 m), 8 (9, 10, 11, 11, 12) balls Butterscotch #189

Crochet hooks, sizes G/6 and H/8 (4.00 and 5.00 mm) or size needed to obtain gauge

Row 2: Hdc into the next 6 sts, BPDC into the next 2 post sts, skip the 2 sts in front of the 2 BPDC just made, hdc into the next 4 hdc, BPDC into the next 4 post sts, skip the 4 sts in front of the 4 BPDC just made, hdc into the next 4 sts, BPDC into the next 2 post sts, skip the 2 sts in front of the 2 BPDC just made, hdc into the next 6 hdc.

Row 3: Rope St, skip the hdc behind the Rope St just made, hdc into the next hdc, PC, hdc into the next hdc, Rope St, skip the hdc behind the Rope St just made, hdc into the next hdc, hdc into the top of the next 2 post sts, FPTR into the same 2 post sts as the last 2 hdc made, FPTR into the next 2 post sts, skip the 4 hdc behind the 4 post sts just made, hdc into the next 4 sts, FPTR into the same 2 post sts as the last 2 hdc made, FPTR into the next 2 post sts, skip the 4 hdc behind the 4 post sts just made, hdc into the next 3 sts, Rope St, skip the hdc behind the Rope St just made, hdc into the next hdc, PC, hdc into the next hdc, Rope St, skip the hdc behind the Rope St just made.

Row 4: Hdc into the next 8 sts, BPDC into the next 4 post sts, skip the 4 hdc in front of the 4 post sts just made, hdc into the next 4 hdc, BPDC into the next 4 post sts, skip the 4 hdc in front of the 4 post sts just made, hdc into the next 8 sts.

Row 5: Rope St, skip the hdc behind the Rope St just made, hdc into the next 3 hdc, Rope St, skip the hdc behind the Rope St just made, hdc into the next hdc, skip the next 2 sts, FPTR into the next 2 post sts, skip the 2 sts behind the 2 FPTR just made, hdc into the next 4 sts, FPTR into the same 2 post sts as the last 2 hdc made, FPTR into the next 2 post sts, skip the 4 hdc behind the 4 post sts just made, hdc into the next 4 sts, FPTR into the same 2 post sts as the last 2 hdc made, skip the next 2 sts, hdc into the next hdc, Rope St, skip the hdc behind the Rope St just made, hdc into the next 3 hdc, Rope St, skip the hdc behind the Rope St just made.

Row 6: Hdc into the next 6 sts, BPDC into the next 2 post sts, skip the 2 hdc in front of the 2 post sts just made, hdc into the next 4 hdc, BPDC into the next 4 post sts, skip the 4 hdc in front of the 4 post sts just made, hdc into the next 4 hdc, BPDC into the next 2 post sts, skip the 2 hdc in front of the 2 post sts just made, hdc into the next 6 sts.

Repeat Rows 3-6 for patt.

SIDEWAYS RIB PATTERN
(any number of sts)

Foundation Row (RS): Sc into second ch from hook and into each ch across. Ch 1, turn.

Patt Row: Sc *through the back loop only* of each sc across. Ch 1, turn.

Repeat Patt Row.

NOTES

Throughout, each hdc, post st, PC, and turning-ch-2 counts as 1 st.

Throughout, each FPDTR, FPTR, and BPDC counts as 1 post st.

FPDTR = (Yarn over hook) 3 times, insert hook *from front to back to front* around the post of indicated stitch, yarn over hook and pull up a loop; (yarn over hook and draw loop through 2 loops on hook) 4 times. Unless noted otherwise, always skip the st behind the FPDTR.

FPTR = (Yarn over hook) twice, insert hook *from front to back to front* around the post of indicated stitch, yarn over hook and pull up a loop; (yarn over hook and draw loop through 2 loops on hook) 3 times. Unless noted otherwise, always skip the st behind the FPTR.

BPDC = Yarn over hook, insert hook *from back to front to back* around the post of indicated stitch, yarn over hook and pull up a loop; (yarn over hook and draw loop through 2 loops on hook) twice. Unless noted otherwise, always skip the st behind the BPDC.

Rope St = [(Yarn over hook) twice, insert hook *from front to back to front* around the post of the st two rows below, yarn over hook and pull up a loop, (yarn over hook and draw loop through 2 loops on hook) twice] *twice,* yarn over hook and draw loop through all 3 loops on hook.

Popcorn = PC = 5 dc into next st, drop loop from hook; insert hook *from front to back* into first dc made, replace loop onto hook and draw loop through.

To decrease 1 st each side, ch 2 to turn; skip first st, work a dec hdc to combine next 2 sts; cont patt as established until 3 sts rem, ending row with dec hdc to combine next 2 sts, hdc into top of turning-ch-2. Ch 2, turn.

To decrease 2 sts each side, ch 2 to turn; skip first st, (work a dec hdc to combine next 2 sts) twice; cont patt as established until 5 sts rem, ending row with (dec hdc to combine next 2 sts) twice, hdc into top of turning-ch-2. Ch 2, turn.

Decrease half double crochet = dec hdc = Yarn over hook, insert hook into next st and pull up a loop (3 loops are on your hook); yarn over hook, insert hook into next st and pull up a loop; yarn over hook and draw loop through all 5 loops on hook.

For sweater assembly, refer to the illustration for set-in construction on page 126.

Shape Armholes

Next Row (RS): Slip st into first 3 (4, 6, 7, 8, 11) sts, ch 2, skip st where last slip st was worked, cont patt as established until 2 (3, 5, 6, 7, 10) sts rem in row. Ch 2, turn, leaving rest of row unworked—70 (76, 80, 86, 92, 94) sts rem.

Cont patts as established, and dec 2 sts each side every row 1 (4, 4, 5, 5, 6) times, then dec 1 st each side every row 6 (3, 4, 5, 7, 6) times—54 (54, 56, 56, 58, 58) sts rem.

Cont even in patts as established until piece measures approx 19 (19¼, 19½, 20, 20½, 20½)" from beg, ending after WS row. Ch 2, turn.

Shape Neck

Work patts as established across first 14 (14, 15, 15, 16, 16) sts. Ch 2, turn, leaving rest of row unworked.

Cont patts as established, and dec 1 st at neck edge once—13 (13, 14, 14, 15, 15) sts rem. Ch 2, turn.

Cont even in patts as established until this side measures approx 20 (20¼, 20½, 21, 21½, 21½)" from beg.

Fasten off.

For second side of neck, with RS facing, skip the middle 26 sts and attach yarn with a slip st to next st and ch 2.

Complete same as first side.

FRONT

Same as back until piece measures approx 17½ (17¾, 18, 18½, 19, 19)" from beg, ending after WS row. Ch 2, turn.

Shape Neck

Next Row (RS): Work patts as established across first 17 (17, 18, 18, 19, 19) sts. Ch 2, turn, leaving rest of row unworked.

Cont patts as established, and dec 1 st at neck edge every row 4 times—13 (13, 14, 14, 15, 15) sts rem. Ch 2, turn.

Cont even in patts as established until this side measures same as back.

Fasten off.

For second side of neck, with RS facing, skip the middle 20 sts, and attach yarn with a slip st to next st and ch 2.

Complete same as first side.

SLEEVES

With larger hook, ch 37.

Foundation Row 1 (RS): Hdc into third ch from hook and into each ch across—36 sts. Ch 2, turn.

Foundation Row 2: Skip first st, hdc into each hdc across, ending row with hdc into top of turning-ch-2—36 sts. Ch 2, turn.

Set Up Patts

Next Row (RS): Skip first st, hdc into the next 3 sts, work Row 1 of Aran Panel Patt over the middle 28 sts, hdc into the next 3 sts, hdc into top of turning-ch-2. Ch 2, turn.

Cont in Solid Hdc Patt with Aran Panel Patt over the middle 28 sts as established, **and at the same time,** inc 1 st each side every other row 0 (1, 2, 4, 6, 6) times, every fourth row 11 (12, 12, 11, 10, 10)

COOL TIP If you'd prefer a crew-neck pullover, just chain 9 instead of chaining 17, and work Sideways Rib Pattern over 8 stitches.

times, then every sixth row 1 (0, 0, 0, 0, 0) times—60 (62, 64, 66, 68, 68) sts.

Cont even, if necessary, in patts as established until piece measures approx 17¾ (17¾, 18¼, 18¼, 18¼, 18¼)" from beg, ending after WS row. *Do not ch 2.* Turn.

Shape Cap

Next Row (RS): Slip st into first 3 (4, 6, 7, 8, 11) sts, ch 2, skip st where last slip st was worked, cont patts as established until 2 (3, 5, 6, 7, 10) sts rem. Ch 2, turn, leaving rest of row unworked.

Cont patts as established, and dec 1 st each side every row 3 (7, 10, 14, 16, 15) times, then dec 2 sts each side every row 8 (6, 4, 2, 1, 0) times—18 sts rem.

Cont even in patts as established for 1 (0, 1, 0, 0, 2) rows. *Do not ch 2.* Turn.

Next Row: Slip st into first 3 sts, ch 2. Skip st where last slip st was worked, hdc into each st across until 2 sts rem—14 sts rem. *Do not ch 2.* Turn.

Next Row: Slip st into first 3 sts, ch 2. Skip st where last slip st was worked, hdc into each st across until 2 sts rem—10 sts.

Fasten off.

FINISHING

Sew shoulder seams.

With RS facing and smaller hook, attach yarn with a slip st to neck edge of left shoulder seam and ch 1.

Work 71 sc evenly spaced around neckline. Join with a slip st to first sc.

Fasten off.

Neckband

With smaller hook, ch 17.

Work even in Sideways Rib Patt on 16 sts until neckband, when slightly stretched, fits around neckline.

Fasten off.

Sew foundation row of neckband to the last row of the neckband. Sew neckband into place onto neckline, placing seam at center of back neck.

Set in sleeves.

Sew side and sleeve seams.

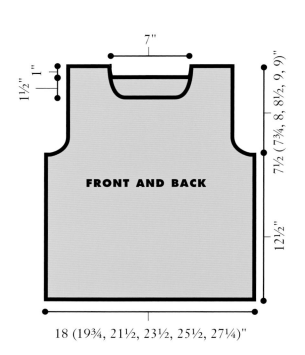

7"

1½" 1"

7½ (7¾, 8, 8½, 9, 9)"

FRONT AND BACK

12½"

18 (19¾, 21½, 23½, 25½, 27¼)"

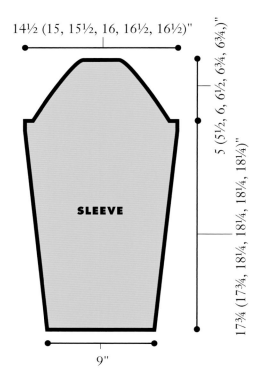

14½ (15, 15½, 16, 16½, 16½)"

5 (5½, 6, 6½, 6¾, 6¾)"

SLEEVE

17¾ (17¾, 18¼, 18¼, 18¼, 18¼)"

9"

Margo

Here's one of those projects that's definitely easier to make than it is to wear—a classic string bikini!

GAUGE

In Solid Sc Patt with larger hook, 20 sts and 22 rows = 4". To measure your gauge, make a test swatch as follows: With larger hook, ch 21. Work Solid Sc Patt on 20 sts for 22 rows total. Fasten off. Piece should measure 4" square. **To save time, take time to check gauge.**

SOLID SINGLE CROCHET PATTERN

(any number of sts)

Foundation Row (RS): Sc into second ch from hook and into each ch across. Ch 1, turn.

Patt Row: Sc into first sc, *sc into next sc. Repeat from * across. Ch 1, turn.

Repeat Patt Row for patt.

NOTES

Throughout, each sc and dec sc counts as 1 st.

To decrease 1 st each side, sc into first sc, dec sc to combine next 2 sts, sc into each st across until 3 sts rem, ending row with dec sc to combine next 2 sts, sc into last sc. Ch 1, turn.

To increase 1 st each side, sc into first sc, 2 sc into next sc, sc into each sc across until 2 sc rem, ending row with 2 sc into next sc, sc into last sc. Ch 1, turn.

Decrease single crochet = dec sc = (Insert hook into next st and pull up a loop) twice, yarn over hook and draw loop through all 3 loops on hook.

RIGHT CUP OF TOP

With larger hook, ch 29 (33, 37).

Beg Solid Sc Patt, and work even on 28 (32, 36) sts for 20 (18, 16) rows total. Ch 1, turn.

Next Row (RS): Sc into first 19 (18, 17) sc. Ch 1, turn, leaving rest of row unworked.

Cont even on 19 (18, 17) sts in patt as established for 8 (13, 19) more rows. Fasten off.

Cut lining for cup, making it ½" larger than the crocheted piece on all sides.

With RS facing, fold crocheted piece, and sew side edges of the last 9 (14, 20) rows to the top of the 9 (14, 19) sts left unworked.

Edging

With RS facing and smaller hook, attach yarn with a slip st to lower right corner of cup and ch 1. Work sc evenly spaced along the side to upper corner.

Make tie as follows: ch 90; slip st into second ch from hook and into next 88 ch; work sc evenly spaced along other side of cup to lower left corner.

SKILL LEVEL
Advanced Beginner

SIZES
Top: Cup Size A (B, C)
Bottom: One size fits all

MATERIALS
Aurora Yarn/Ornaghi Filati's *Muskat* (light worsted weight; 100% Egyptian cotton; each approx 1¾ oz/ 50 g and 110 yd/100 m, 4 (5, 5) balls Ocean Blue #203

Crochet hooks, sizes E/4 and F/5 (3.50 and 3.75 mm) or size needed to obtain gauge

Elastic, ¼" wide, approx 1 yd

Fabric for lining, approx ½ yd

Matching sewing thread

At lower left corner of cup, ch 4. Working along bottom of cup, work (dc, ch 1) into every other row and into every other st along lower edge. Ch 4, join with a slip st to first sc. Fasten off.

LEFT CUP OF TOP

With larger hook, ch 29 (33, 37).

Beg Solid Sc Patt, and work even on 28 (32, 36) sts for 20 (18, 16) rows total. Fasten off.

Next Row (RS): With RS facing, skip the first 9 (14, 19) sc, and attach yarn with a slip st to next st and ch 1, sc into next 19 (18, 17) sts. Ch 1, turn.

Cont even on 19 (18, 17) sts in patt as established for 8 (13, 19) more rows. Fasten off.

Cut lining as for right cup.

With RS facing, fold cup and sew side edges of the last 9 (14, 20) rows to the top of the 9 (14, 19) sts left unworked.

Edging
Same as edging for right cup.

Finishing of Top
Fold ½" of lining under and pin to WS of cups, allowing extra fabric at dart to form a pleat.

Whipstitch linings into place.

Tie
Ch 270.

Slip st into second ch from hook and into each ch across. Fasten off.

Weave tie through ch-1 spaces along bottom of cups.

BOTTOM

Begin with back, and with larger hook, ch 65.

Beg Solid Sc Patt, and work even on 64 sts for 6 rows total. Ch 1, turn.

Dec 1 st each side every fourth row 6 times, every other row 11 times, then every row 9 times—12 sts rem. Ch 1, turn.

For crotch, cont even on 12 sts in patt as established for 16 rows. Ch 1, turn.

For front, inc 1 st each side every other row 15 times, then every fourth row 3 times—48 sts. Ch 1, turn.

Cont even in patt as established for 6 rows. Fasten off.

Cut lining, making it ½" larger than the crocheted piece on all sides.

Right Leg Opening Edging
With RS facing and smaller hook, attach yarn with a slip st to upper right front edge and ch 1.

Work 92 sc evenly spaced along right side of bottom. Fasten off.

Left Leg Opening Edging
With RS facing and smaller hook, attach yarn with a slip st to upper left back edge and ch 1.

Complete same as right leg opening edging.

Back Ties
With smaller hook, ch 70.

Slip st into second ch from hook and into next 68 ch; with RS of back facing and working into unused loops of foundation chain, sc into next 64 sts of back; ch 70, turn, slip st into second ch from hook and into next 68 ch. Join with a slip st to last sc. Fasten off.

Front Ties
With smaller hook, ch 70.

Slip st into second ch from hook and into next 68 ch; with RS of front facing, sc into next 48 sts of front; ch 70, turn, slip st into second ch from hook and into next 68 ch. Join with a slip st to last sc. Fasten off.

Finishing of Bottom
With WS facing, whipstitch elastic into place approx ¼" from side edges of bottom, stretching elastic slightly.

Fold edges of lining ½" under on all sides, and pin to WS of bottom to cover elastic.

Whipstitch lining into place.

COOL TIP It's easier to pin the lining into the bikini top if the cups are inside out.

Traci

Crocheted in the round from the top down, this cozy hat is quick and fun to make. Once you get it started, I bet you'll want to keep on going until it's completed. Your fingers will fly through these short fourteen rounds!

GAUGE

In Solid Dc Pattern, 9 dc and 6 rows = 4". To measure your gauge, make a test swatch as follows: Ch 11.

Foundation Row (RS): Dc into fourth ch from hook and into each ch across. Ch 3, turn.

Next Row: Skip first dc, *dc into next dc. Repeat from * across, ending row with dc into top of turning-ch-3. Ch 3, turn.

Repeat last row 4 more times.

Fasten off.

Piece should measure 4" square. **To save time, take time to check gauge.**

NOTES

Throughout, each dc and ch-3 counts as 1 st.

Since this hat is worked in the round, RS always faces you.

HAT

Ch 3. Join with a slip st to form a ring.

Rnd 1 (RS): Ch 3, 11 dc into ring—12 sts. Join with a slip st to top of ch-3.

Rnd 2: Ch 3, dc into same st as slip st, (2 dc into next dc) 11 times—24 sts. Join with a slip st to top of ch-3.

Rnd 3: Ch 3, *2 dc into next dc, dc into next dc. Repeat from * around, ending rnd with 2 dc into next dc—36 sts. Join with a slip st to top of ch-3.

Rnd 4: Ch 3, dc into next dc, *2 dc into next dc, dc into next 2 dc. Repeat from * around, ending rnd with 2 dc into next dc—48 sts. Join with a slip st to top of ch-3.

Rnd 5: Ch 3, *dc into next dc. Repeat from * around—48 sts. Join with a slip st to top of ch-3.

Rnds 6-12: Same as Rnd 5—48 sts. Join with a slip st to top of ch-3.

Rnd 13: Ch 3, dc into same st as slip st, *2 dc into next dc, dc into next dc. Repeat from * around, ending rnd with 2 dc into next dc—72 sts. Join with a slip st to top of ch-3.

Rnd 14: Same as Rnd 13—108 sts. Join with a slip st to top of ch-3.

Fasten off.

SKILL LEVEL
Intermediate

SIZES
One size fits all

MATERIALS
Coats and Clark's *TLC Macaroon* (bulky weight; 100% polyester; each approx 3 oz/85 g and 115 yd/105 m), 1 skein Granite #9317

Crochet hook, size K/10.5 (6.50 mm) or size needed to obtain gauge

COOL TIP To make a summer version of this hat, crochet it using several strands of linen or cotton yarn held together. To ensure a perfect fit, be certain to measure your gauge before you start.

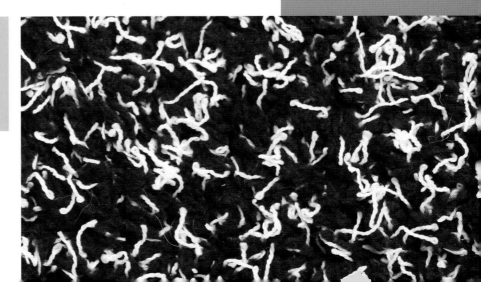

Toni

A dramatic neckline sets this textured pullover apart. Its fold-over collar will frame your face beautifully.

GAUGE

In Textured Patt, 16 sts and 11 rows = 4". To measure your gauge, make a test swatch as follows: With A, ch 19. Work Textured Patt on 17 sts for 11 rows total. Fasten off. Piece should measure 4¼" wide and 4" high. **To save time, take time to check gauge.**

TEXTURED PATTERN
(mult 2 + 1 sts)

Foundation Row (RS): Dc into fourth ch from hook and into each ch across. Change color, ch 1, turn.

Row 1 (WS): Sc into first dc, *BPDC into next dc, sc into next dc. Repeat from * across, ending row with BPDC into next dc, sc into top of turning-ch-3. Change color, ch 3, turn.

Row 2: Skip first sc, *dc into next st. Repeat from * across. Change color, ch 1, turn.

Repeat Rows 1 and 2 in Stripe Patt for patt.

STRIPE PATTERN

One row *each* of *A, B, C, A, D, E. Repeat from * for patt.

NOTES

Throughout, each sc, dc, BPDC, dec sc, dec dc, and turning-ch-3 counts as 1 st.

To change color, work the last stitch of the first color until 2 loops remain on your hook, then yarn over hook with the new color and complete the stitch.

Continued on next page.

BACK

With A, ch 73 (81, 91, 101, 111).

Beg Textured Patt, and work even on 71 (79, 89, 99, 109) sts in Stripe Patt until piece measures approx 12¾" from beg, ending after Row 1 of patt.

Fasten off.

Shape Raglan

With RS facing, skip first 4 (4, 4, 6, 8) sts, and attach yarn with a slip st to next st and ch 3. Skip st where last slip st was worked, dc into next st and into each st across until 4 (4, 4, 6, 8) sts rem in row. Change color. Turn, leaving rest of row unworked.

Cont patts as established, and dec 1 st each side every other row 7 (4, 2, 0, 0) times, then every row 9 (16, 23, 28, 31) times—31 sts rem.

Fasten off.

FRONT

Same as back until piece measures approx 19¼ (19¾, 20¾, 21¼, 21¾)" from beg, ending after WS row—41 sts rem. Change color, ch 3, turn.

SKILL LEVEL
Intermediate

SIZES
Small (Medium, Large, Extra-Large, Extra-Extra-Large). *Instructions are for smallest size, with changes for other sizes noted in parentheses as necessary.*

FINISHED MEASUREMENTS
Bust: 35½ (39½, 44½, 49½, 54½)"
Total length: 22¼ (22¾, 23¾, 24¼, 24¾)"

MATERIALS
Lion Brand's *Wool-Ease* (worsted weight; 80% acrylic/20% wool; each approx 3 oz/85 g and 197 yd/180 m), 3 (4, 4, 5, 5) balls Black #153 (A), and 2 (2, 3, 3, 4) skeins *each* of Colonial Blue #117 (B), Turquoise #148 (C), Peacock #170 (D), and Delft #116 (E)

Crochet hook, size H/8 (5.00 mm) or size needed to obtain gauge

Back Post Double Crochet = BPDC = Yarn over hook, insert hook *from back to front to back* around the post of indicated stitch, yarn over hook and pull up a loop; (yarn over hook and draw loop through 2 loops on hook) twice. Unless noted otherwise, always skip the st behind the BPDC.

To increase, work 2 sts into 1 st.

To decrease on Row 1 of Textured Patt when sc is the first and last st in the row: Ch 1 to turn, then work a dec sc to combine the first 2 sts in row, *sc into next st, BPDC into next st. Repeat from * across until 3 sts rem, ending row with sc into next st, dec sc to combine the last 2 sts in row.

To decrease on Row 1 of Textured Patt when BPDC is the first and last st in the row: Ch 1 to turn, work a dec sc to combine the first 2 sts in row, *BPDC into next st, sc into next st. Repeat from * across until 3 sts rem, ending row with BPDC into next st, dec sc to combine the last 2 sts in row.

To decrease on Row 2 of Textured Patt when dc is the first and last st in the row: Ch 3 to turn, skip the first st, then work a dec dc to combine the next 2 sts in row, cont across row until 3 sts rem, ending row with a dec dc to combine the next 2 sts, dc into last st in row.

Decrease single crochet = dec sc = (Insert hook into next st and pull up a loop) twice, yarn over hook and draw loop through all 3 loops on hook.

Decrease double crochet = dec dc = Yarn over hook, insert hook into next st and pull up a loop (3 loops are on your hook); yarn over hook and draw loop through 2 loops on hook (2 loops are on your hook); yarn over hook, insert hook into next st and pull up a loop (4 loops are on your hook); yarn over hook and draw loop through 2 loops on hook; yarn over hook and draw loop through all 3 loops on hook.

For sweater assembly, refer to the illustration for raglan construction on page 126.

Shape Neck

Next Row (RS): Skip the first st, then work a dec dc to combine the next 2 sts, cont across next 6 sts. Change color, turn.

Cont raglan shaping same as back, *and at the same time,* dec 1 st at neck edge every row 4 times.

For second side of neck, with RS facing, skip the middle 23 sts, and attach yarn with a slip st to next st and ch 3.

Complete same as first side.

SLEEVES

With A, ch 39 (41, 43, 45, 45).

Beg Textured Patt, and work even on 37 (39, 41, 43, 43) sts in Stripe Patt for 2 rows.

Cont patts as established, and inc 1 st each side every other row 0 (0, 0, 2, 10) times, every fourth row 2 (5, 11, 10, 6) times, then every sixth row 6 (4, 0, 0, 0) times—53 (57, 63, 67, 75) sts.

Cont even in patts as established until piece measures approx 17" from beg, ending after WS row.

Fasten off.

Shape Raglan

With RS facing, skip first 4 (4, 4, 6, 8) sts, attach yarn with a slip st to next st and ch 3. Skip st where last slip st was worked, dc into next st and into each st across until 4 (4, 4, 6, 8) sts rem in row. Change color. Turn, leaving rest of row unworked.

Cont patts as established, and dec 1 st each side every other row 5 (4, 4, 5, 6) times, then every row 13 (16, 19, 18, 19) times—9 sts rem.

Fasten off.

FINISHING

Collar

With A, ch 20.

Dc into fourth ch from hook and into next 16 ch, with WS facing, work 9 dc along top of one sleeve, 31 dc along back of neck, 9 dc along top of second sleeve, 9 dc along shaped edge of front neck, 22 dc along center of neckline, 9 dc along shaped edge of front neck—107 sts total.

Cont even in Textured Patt and Stripe Patt until collar measures approx 7½" from beg, ending after a row worked with A.

Fasten off.

Sew the 18-st extension under the collar onto front neck edge.

Sew raglan seams. Sew side and sleeve seams.

COOL TIP Want to minimize the number of yarn tails you must weave in? Don't cut Color A after each stripe; instead, carry it *loosely* up the side of the fabric until it is needed again!

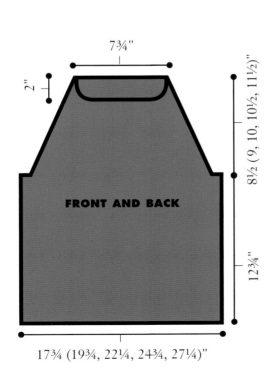

7¾"

2"

FRONT AND BACK

8½ (9, 10, 10½, 11½)"

12¾"

17¾ (19¾, 22¼, 24¾, 27¼)"

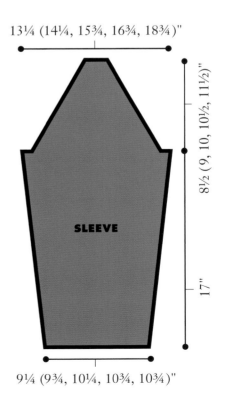

13¼ (14¼, 15¾, 16¾, 18¾)"

8½ (9, 10, 10½, 11½)"

SLEEVE

17"

9¼ (9¾, 10¼, 10¾, 10¾)"

Anika

Sexy yet demure, this trendy top features openwork bell sleeves on a cropped, opaque body.

GAUGE

In Solid Dc Patt, 20 sts and 10 rows = 4". To measure your gauge, make a test swatch as follows: Ch 22. Work Solid Dc Patt on 20 sts for 10 rows total. Fasten off. Piece should measure 4" square. **To save time, take time to check gauge.**

SOLID DOUBLE CROCHET PATTERN

(any number of sts)

Foundation Row (RS): Dc into fourth ch from hook and into each ch across. Ch 3, turn.

Patt Row: Skip first dc, *dc into next dc. Repeat from * across, ending row with dc into top of turning-ch-3. Ch 3, turn.

Repeat Patt Row for patt.

OPEN V-STITCH PATTERN

(mult 3 + 2 sts)

Foundation Row (RS): Open V-St into fifth ch from hook, *skip next 2 ch, Open V-St into next ch. Repeat from * across, ending row with skip next ch, dc into last ch. Ch 3, turn.

Patt Row: Skip first dc, *Open V-St into next ch-2 sp. Repeat from * across, ending row with dc into top of turning-ch-3. Ch 3, turn.

Repeat Patt Row.

NOTES

Throughout, each dc, ch-1 sp, and turning-ch-3 counts as 1 st; each Open V-St counts as 3 sts.

Open V-St = (Dc, ch 2, dc) into indicated st.

Continued on next page.

BACK

Ch 88 (98, 108, 120, 134).

Beg Solid Dc Patt, and work even on 86 (96, 106, 118, 132) sts until piece measures approx 8" from beg. *Do not ch 3.* Turn.

Shape Raglan

Next Row (RS): Slip st into first 9 sts, ch 3, skip st where last slip st was worked, dc into each st across until 8 sts rem in row. Turn, leaving rest of row unworked—70 (80, 90, 102, 116) sts rem.

Cont Solid Dc Patt as established, and dec 2 sts each side every row 0 (0, 2, 7, 13) times, dec 1 st each side every row 12 (21, 22, 18, 13) times, then dec 1 st each side every other row 4 (0, 0, 0, 0) times—38 sts rem. Fasten off.

FRONT

Same as back until piece measures approx 12¾ (13¼, 14¼, 14¾, 15¼)" from beg, ending after WS (RS, WS, RS, WS) row—46 (54, 54, 54, 54) sts rem. Ch 3, turn.

SKILL LEVEL
Intermediate

SIZES
Small (Medium, Large, Extra-Large, Extra-Extra-Large). *Instructions are for smallest size, with changes for other sizes noted in parentheses as necessary.*

FINISHED MEASUREMENTS
Bust: 34½ (38½, 42½, 47, 53)"
Total length: 18½ (19, 20, 20½, 21)"

MATERIALS
Plymouth Yarn's *Wildflower* (light worsted weight; 51% cotton/49% acrylic; each approx 1¾ oz/50 g and 136 yd/124 m), 10 (11, 12, 13, 14) balls Magenta #75

Crochet hook, size E/4 (3.50 mm) or size needed to obtain gauge

To decrease 1 st each side in Solid Dc Patt: Ch 3 to turn, skip first dc, work a dec dc to combine the next 2 dc, cont across until 3 sts rem in row, ending row with dec dc to combine the next 2 dc, dc into top of turning-ch-3. Ch 3, turn.

To decrease 2 sts each side in Solid Dc Patt: Ch 3 to turn, skip first dc, (work a dec dc to combine the next 2 dc) twice, cont across until 5 sts rem in row, ending row with (dec dc to combine the next 2 dc) twice, dc into top of turning-ch-3. Ch 3, turn.

Decrease double crochet = dec dc = Yarn over hook, insert hook into next st and pull up a loop (3 loops are on your hook); yarn over hook and draw loop through 2 loops on hook (2 loops are on your hook); yarn over hook, insert hook into next st and pull up a loop (4 loops are on your hook); yarn over hook and draw loop through 2 loops on hook; yarn over hook and draw loop through all 3 loops on hook.

Decrease double-triple crochet = dec dc-tr = Yarn over hook, insert hook into first dc of next Open V-St and pull up a loop, yarn over hook and draw loop through 2 loops on hook, (yarn over hook) twice and insert hook into top of turning-ch and pull up a loop, (yarn over hook and draw loop through 2 loops on hook) twice, yarn over hook and draw loop through all 3 loops on hook.

Reverse Single Crochet = reverse sc = *Working from left to right,* sc into each sc.

For sweater assembly, refer to the illustration for raglan construction on page 126.

Shape Neck

For Size Small Only:
Next Row: Skip first st, cont across next 11 sts. Ch 3, turn, leaving rest of row unworked.

For Sizes Medium, Large, Extra-Large, and Extra-Extra-Large Only:
Next Row: Skip the first st, then work a dec dc to combine the next 2 sts, cont across next 12 sts. Ch 3, turn, leaving rest of row unworked.

For All Sizes:
Cont raglan shaping same as back, **and at the same time,** dec 1 st at neck edge every row 5 times—4 sts rem this side. Ch 3, turn.

Next Row (RS): Skip first st, work a dec dc to combine the next 2 sts, dc into top of turning-ch-3—3 sts rem this side. Ch 3, turn.

Next Row: Skip first st, work a dec dc to combine the next 2 sts. Fasten off.

For second side of neck, with RS (WS, RS, WS, RS) facing, skip the middle 24 sts, and attach yarn with a slip st to next st and ch 3.

Complete same as first side.

SLEEVES

Ch 79 (79, 85, 97, 97).

Beg Open V-St Patt, and work even for 12 (20, 20, 12, 12) rows—25 (25, 27, 31, 31) Open V-Sts plus 1 dc each side. After last row, ch 4, turn.

Decrease Row (RS): Skip first 2 dc and ch-2 sp, dc into next dc, *Open V-St into next ch-2 sp. Repeat from * across until 1 Open V-St plus 1 dc rem in row, ending row with dec dc-tr to combine the first dc of next Open V-St and the turning-ch. Ch 3, turn.

Next Row: Skip first dec dc-tr, *Open V-St into next ch-2 sp. Repeat from * across, ending row with dc into top of turning-ch. Ch 3, turn.

Cont even in patt as established for 11 (19, 19, 11, 11) rows. After last row, ch 4, turn.

Work Decrease Row once—21 (21, 23, 27, 27) Open V-Sts plus 1 dc each side.

Cont even in patt as established for 11 (19, 19, 11, 11) rows. After last row, ch 4, turn.

For Sizes Small, Extra-Large, and Extra-Extra-Large Only:
Work Decrease Row once—19 (_, _, 25, 25) Open V-Sts plus 1 dc each side.

For All Sizes:

Cont even in patt as established until piece measures approx 17½" from beg, ending after WS row. *Do not ch 3.* Turn.

Shape Raglan

Next Row (RS): Slip st into first 2 dc, 2 slip sts into next ch-2 sp, slip st into next 2 dc, 2 slip sts into next ch-2 sp, slip st into next dc, ch 3, *Open V-St into next ch-2 sp. Repeat from * across until 2 Open V-Sts plus 1 dc rem in row, ending row with dc into first dc of next Open V-St—15 (17, 19, 21, 21) Open V-Sts plus 1 dc each side. Ch 3, turn.

Cont even in patt as established for 3 rows. After last row, ch 4, turn.

Decrease Row 1 (RS): Skip first 2 dc and ch-2 sp, dc into next dc, *Open V-St into next ch-2 sp. Repeat from * across until 1 Open V-St plus 1 dc rem in row, ending row with dec dc-tr to combine the first dc of next Open V-St and the turning-ch. Ch 3, turn.

Decrease Row 2: Skip first dec dc-tr, *Open V-St into next ch-2 sp. Repeat from * across, ending row with dc into top of turning-ch. Ch 3, turn.

Cont even in patt as established for 2 rows. After last row, ch 4, turn.

Repeat last 4 rows 3 (2, 3, 2, 2) more times, then work Decrease Row 1 once more—5 (9, 9, 13, 13) Open V-Sts plus 1 dc each side. Ch 3, turn.

Repeat Decrease Rows 1 and 2 0 (2, 2, 4, 4) times— 5 Open V-Sts plus 1 dc each side.

Cont even in patt as established for 0 (1, 0, 1, 2) rows. Fasten off.

FINISHING

Sew raglan seams.

Neckline Edging

Rnd 1 (RS): With RS facing, attach yarn with a slip st to left back raglan seam and ch 1. Work 134 sc evenly spaced around neckline. Join with a slip st to first sc. Ch 1.

Rnd 2 (RS): Work reverse sc into each sc around. Join with a slip st to first sc. Fasten off.

Sew side and sleeve seams.

Lower Edging

Rnd 1 (RS): With RS facing, attach yarn with a slip st to left side seam and ch 1. Working into unused loops of foundation ch, work 172 (192, 212, 236, 264) sc evenly spaced around lower edge. Join with a slip st to first sc. Ch 1.

Rnd 2 (RS): Work reverse sc into each sc around. Join with a slip st to first sc. Fasten off.

Sleeve Edging

Rnd 1 (RS): With RS facing, attach yarn with a slip st to lower sleeve seam and ch 1. Working into unused loops of foundation ch, sc into same ch as slip st, *sc into next ch-sp, sc into same ch as next Open V-St. Repeat from * across, ending rnd with sc into next ch-sp, slip st to first sc. Ch 1.

Rnd 2 (RS): Work reverse sc into each sc around. Join with a slip st to first sc. Fasten off.

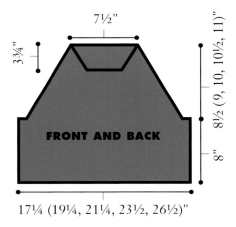

7½"
3¾"
8½ (9, 10, 10½, 11)"
8"
FRONT AND BACK
17¼ (19¼, 21¼, 23½, 26½)"

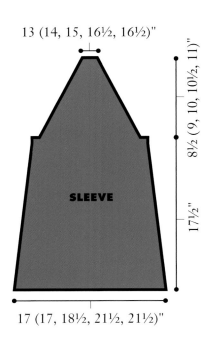

13 (14, 15, 16½, 16½)"
8½ (9, 10, 10½, 11)"
17½"
SLEEVE
17 (17, 18½, 21½, 21½)"

Basic Stitches

Chain (ch)

Place a slip knot on your hook. Yarn over hook and draw loop through the loop on the hook to form the first chain. Repeat this step as many times as required. *Note:* In patterns, the loop on the hook is *not* included when counting the number of chain stitches.

Slip Stitch (slip st)

Insert hook into the indicated stitch, yarn over hook and draw loop through both the stitch and the loop on the hook.

Often, a slip stitch is used to form a ring in order to work in the round. To do so, make a foundation chain as specified in the instructions and then work a slip stitch into the first chain to create a ring.

Single Crochet (sc)

Insert hook into indicated stitch, yarn over hook and pull up a loop (2 loops are on your hook); yarn over hook and draw loop through both loops on hook.

Half Double Crochet (hdc)

Yarn over hook, insert hook into indicated stitch (*see* 1), yarn over hook and pull up a loop (3 loops are on your hook); yarn over hook and draw loop through all 3 loops on hook (*see* 2).

Double Crochet (dc)

Yarn over hook, insert hook into indicated stitch (*see* 1), yarn over hook and pull up a loop (3 loops are on your hook); yarn over hook and draw loop through

2 loops on hook (*see* 2); yarn over hook and draw loop through remaining 2 loops on hook (*see* 3).

Triple Crochet (tr)

(Yarn over hook) twice, insert hook into indicated stitch (*see* 1), yarn over hook and pull up a loop (4 loops are on your hook); yarn over hook and draw loop through 2 loops on hook (*see* 2) (3 loops are on your hook); yarn over hook and draw loop through 2 loops on hook (*see* 3); yarn over hook and draw loop through remaining 2 loops on hook (*see* 4).

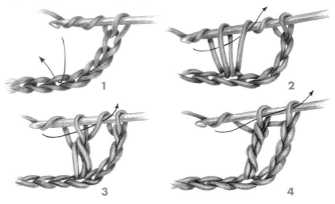

Double Triple Crochet (dtr)

(Yarn over hook) 3 times, insert hook into indicated stitch (*see* 1) and pull up a loop (5 loops are on your hook); yarn over hook and draw loop through 2 loops on hook (*see* 2) (4 loops are on your hook); yarn over hook and draw loop through 2 loops on hook (*see* 3) (3 loops are on your hook); yarn over hook and draw loop through 2 loops on hook (*see* 4); yarn over hook and draw loop through remaining 2 loops on hook (*see* 5).

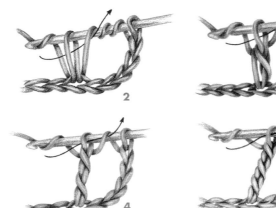

Stitch Variations

Bead Chain (bead ch)
Move a bead up next to the hook, yarn over hook and draw loop through the loop on the hook, locking bead into the stitch.

Long Double Crochet (long dc)
Elongated double crochet stitch worked into the next stitch *two rows below,* pulling up the first loop until it is even with hook.

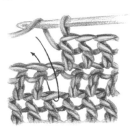

Working around the front post of a stitch (as for Front Post Double Crochet (FPDC) or Front Post Triple Crochet (FPTR) stitches)
Instead of working stitch into the top of the row below, insert hook *from front to back to front* around the post of indicated stitch in the row.

Working around the back post of a stitch (as for Back Post Double Crochet (BPDC) or Back Post Triple Crochet (BPTR) stitches)
Instead of working stitch into the top of the row below, insert hook *from back to front to back* around the post of indicated stitch in the row below.

Decrease Single Crochet (dec sc)
(Insert hook into next stitch and pull up a loop) twice, yarn over hook and draw loop through all 3 loops on hook.

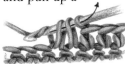

Decrease Half Double Crochet (dec hdc)
(Yarn over hook, insert hook into next stitch and pull up a loop) twice, yarn over hook and draw loop through all 5 loops on hook.

Decrease Double Crochet (dec dc)
(Yarn over hook, insert hook into next stitch, yarn over hook and pull up a loop, yarn over hook and draw loop through 2 loops on hook) twice, yarn over hook and draw loop through all 3 loops on hook.

Reverse Single Crochet (reverse sc)
Working from left to right, insert hook into next stitch (*see* 1), yarn over hook and pull up a loop; yarn over hook and draw loop through both loops on hook (*see* 2). Continue across, moving from left to right across the crocheted fabric (*see* 3).

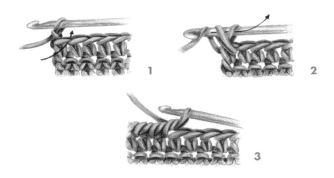

Working into the back or front loop only
Instead of working into both loops of the indicated stitch, insert the hook *under the back or front loop only.*

Working into both loops

Working into the back loop only

Working into the front loop only

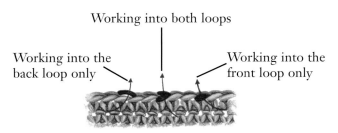

Sweater Assembly

Pieces for crocheted garments fit together like a jig-saw puzzle, with the type of armhole determining how the front, back, and sleeves interlock. Refer to the drawings below when assembling sweaters.

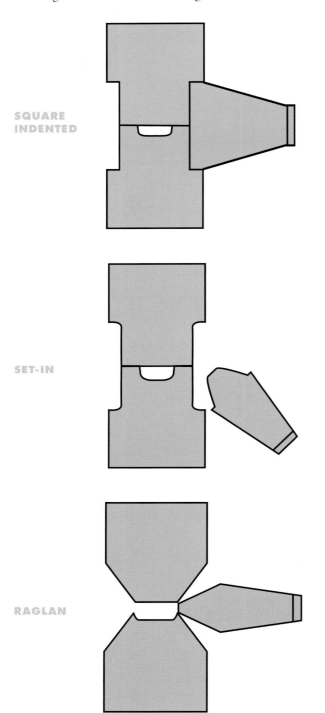

SQUARE
INDENTED

SET-IN

RAGLAN

Finishing Techniques

Whipstitch Seam
With pieces laying flat with RS facing, sew *through back loops only* as shown in illustration.

Mattress Stitch Seam
For invisible vertical seam (such as side and sleeve seams):

- With RS facing, pin the two pieces together, carefully matching patterns and stripes.

- Thread a tapestry needle with your yarn. Bring the needle up from back to front through the lower RH corner of the LH piece of fabric, leaving a 6" tail.

- Bring the yarn up and through the bottom edge of the first stitch on the RH piece to secure the lower edges.

- Bring the yarn up and through the first stitch on the LH piece *from front to back to front*. It is usually best to actually go into strands in the center of the stitch in order to form a sturdy seam.

- Insert the needle into the corresponding place on the RH piece *from front to back to front*.

- Repeat the last two steps (*see* **1** *and* **2**), catching the side stitches of each piece until the seam is completed. After you have joined several rows, pull tautly on the seaming yarn, allowing one half of each edge stitch to roll to the WS to form a seam.

- Weave in tails on WS of work.

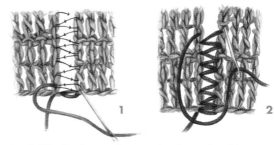

For invisible horizontal seam (such as shoulder seams):
Work the same as vertical seam, except insert the tapestry needle into the top of the stitches on the last row of the two pieces you are seaming (*see* **1** *and* **2**).

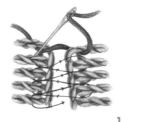 

1   2

Buttonholes

It's easy to add buttonholes to crocheted pieces.

- Work to the place where a buttonhole is to be placed.

- Crochet a number of chains equal to the diameter of the button.

- Skip the same number of stitches on the band as you've chained.

- On the subsequent row, insert your hook *into the chain-space* rather than into the individual chains to crochet the required number of stitches into the buttonhole.

Applying Fringe

- Cut a piece of cardboard to your desired fringe length.

- Wind the yarn *loosely* around the cardboard several times, then cut across one end.

- With the RS of your crocheted fabric facing you, fold several strands of yarn in half and use a crochet hook to loop them onto the edge of your project.

- Pull the loose ends through the folded loop.

- Trim fringe evenly.

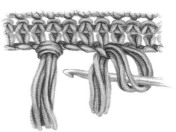

Material Resources

Manufacturers
(These companies sell whole-sale only. Contact them to locate retail stores in your area.)

Artbeads.com
5790 Soundview Drive
Suite 201
Gig Harbor, WA 98335
(253) 857-3433
www.artbeads.com

Aurora Yarns
2385 Carlos Street
P.O. Box 3068
Moss Beach, CA 94038
(650) 728-2730
www.garnstudio.com

Blue Moon Beads
7855 Hayvenhurst Avenue
Van Nuys, CA 91406
(818) 988-8282
www.bluemoonbeads.com

Blue Sky Alpacas
P.O. Box 387
St. Francis, MN 55070
(888) 460-8862
www.blueskyalpacas.com

Brown Sheep Company
100662 County Road 16
Mitchell, NE 69357
(308) 635-2198
www.brownsheep.com

Cascade Yarns
1224 Andover Park East
Tukwilla, WA 98188
(800) 548-1048
www.cascadeyarns.com

Classic Elite Yarns
122 Western Avenue
Lowell, MA 01851
(800) 343-0308
www.classiceliteyarns.com

Coats and Clark
8 Shelter Drive
Greer, SC 29650
(800) 648-1479
www.coatsandclark.com

Dale of Norway
N16 W23390 Stone
    Ridge Drive, #A
Waukesha, WI 53188
(262) 544-1996

JHB International Buttons
1955 South Quince Street
Denver, CO 80231
(800) 525-9007
www.buttons.com

Judi & Co.
18 Gallatin Drive
Dix Hills, NY 11746
(631) 499-8480
www.judiandco.com

Lion Brand Yarn
34 West 15th Street
New York, NY 10011
(212) 243-8995
www.lionbrand.com

Muench Yarns
1323 Scott Street
Petaluma, CA 94954
(800) 733-9276
www.muenchyarns.com

Ornaghi Filati
(*See* Aurora Yarns)

Patons Yarns
320 Livingstone Avenue
    South
Listowel, Ontario
    N4W 3H3
Canada
(519) 291-3780
www.patonsyarns.com

Plymouth Yarns
P.O. Box 28
500 Lafayette Street
Bristol, PA 19007
(215) 788-0459
www.plymouthyarn.com

Tahki/Stacy Charles
70-30 80th Street
Building #36
Ridgewood, NY 11385
(718) 326-4433
www.tahkistacycharles.com

Trendsetter Yarns
16745 Saticoy Street, #101
Van Nuys, CA 91406
(818) 780-5497

**Mail Order and
    Internet Yarn Sources**

Herrschner's and
    Herrschner's Yarn
    Shoppe
2800 Hoover Road
Stevens Point, WI 54492
(800) 441-0838
www.herrschners.com

Patternworks
Route 25
P.O. Box 1618
Center Harbor, NH 03226
(800) 438-5464
www.patternworks.com

Ram Wools
1266 Fife Street
Winnipeg, Manitoba
    R2X 2N6
Canada
(800) 263-8002
www.ramwools.com

Wool Connection
34 East Main Street
Avon, CT 06001
(800) 933-9665
www.woolconnection.com

Instructional and Inspirational Resources

For further technical information, refer to one of the following books:

Brown, Nancy. *The Crocheter's Companion.* Loveland, CO: Interweave Press, 2002.

Goldberg, Rhoda Ochser. *The New Crochet Dictionary.* New York: Crown, 1986.

Kooler, Donna. *Encyclopedia of Crochet.* Little Rock, AR: Leisure Arts, 2002.

Leapman, Melissa. *Cozy Crochet.* San Francisco, CA: Chronicle Books, 2004.

___. *Crochet with Style.* Newtown, CT: Taunton Press, 2000.

___. *Seasons of Love: Crocheted Sweaters for the Family.* Little Rock, AR: Leisure Arts, 2001.

Manthey, Karen, and Susan Brittain. *Crocheting for Dummies.* Hoboken, NJ: Wiley Publishing, 2004.

Mountford, Debra, ed. *The Harmony Guide to Crocheting Techniques and Stitches.* New York: Harmony, 1992.

Righetti, Maggie. *Crocheting in Plain English.* New York: St. Martins Press, 1988.

Thomas, Nancy J. *Knitting and Crocheting* (Barnes and Noble Basics Series). New York: Barnes and Noble, 2004.

Threads editors. *Knitting Tips and Trade Secrets.* Newtown, CT: Taunton Press, 1996.

Tracy, Gloria, and Susan Levin. *Crochet Your Way.* Newtown, CT: Taunton Press, 2000.

To meet other crocheters and to learn more about the craft, contact:

Crochet Guild of America (CGOA)
P.O. Box 3388
Zanesville, OH 43702-3388
(877) 852-9190
e-mail: cgoa@crochet.org
Web site: www.crochet.org

Index